JOHN MAIN:

The Expanding Vision

Edited by
Laurence Freeman
and Stefan Reynolds

CANTERBURY
PRESS
Norwich

First published in 2009 by the Canterbury Press Norwich
Editorial office
13–17 Long Lane,
London, EC1A 9PN, UK

Canterbury Press is an imprint of Hymns Ancient and Modern Ltd
(a registered charity)
St Mary's Works, St Mary's Plain,
Norwich, NR3 3BH, UK

www.scm-canterburypress.co.uk

British Library Cataloguing in Publication data

A catalogue record for this book is available
from the British Library

978 1 85311 943 9

Typeset by Regent Typesetting, London
Printed in the UK by
CPI William Clowes Beccles NR34 7TL

CONTENTS

ACKNOWLEDGEMENTS

My thanks as Editor on behalf of The World Community for Christian Meditation to Mark and Polly Schofield, Fred and Magda Jass, Irene and Luigi Armano and all the Montreal Community who organized the 2007 John Main Seminar from whose proceedings this book has taken form. Special thanks to Susan Spence for help with this project. Thanks also to Beth Cardone for administrative help and Kathleen Carroll for her dedicated work of transcription on this and many other projects. The editorial team at Canterbury Press have again been professional and friendly collaborators. The chapter 'From John Cassian to John Main: Reflections on Christian Meditation' first appeared in *Monastic Studies* 14, Benedictine Priory of Montreal, 1984.

INTRODUCTION

Laurence Freeman

In 1977 John Main arrived in Montreal at the invitation of the Archbishop to establish a Benedictine community grounded in the traditional monastic balance of prayer, work and study, and also in the practice of meditation. The work of the community was to teach meditation by example and participation as well as by words. It was a risk taken in faith, something John Main was good at. Some years after his death this community evolved into what was later christened The World Community for Christian Meditation, a monastery without walls that is now present in more than a hundred countries. As I continue to witness the growth in depth and expansion in outreach of this, a new kind of contemplative community, I often remember scenes from those early years which return with a symbolic charge to illuminate the meaning of John Main's gift to the world.

Meeting recently with a group of young meditators I was struck again by the distance that has opened up between traditional Christian language and ritual and the spirituality of the young. I was reminded of a morning in the early days of the Montreal community when we were working on the house we had been given. A plumber arrived and John Main showed him the work that was to be done. The plumber was a chatty fellow and asked what the house was all about. With characteristic patience and presence Fr John explained what we were doing. The plumber responded with further questions and then with his life history

and the reasons why he no longer went to church and felt alienated from religious people. The discussion went on for a while
and I left to get on with my work. As he was leaving a little later,
I met the plumber again who seemed in a different, more reflect-
ive mood. He remarked what a special moment it had been for
him to talk with Fr John, what an unusual priest he was, and how
grateful he was for the attention and time he had been given. A
few days later I noticed him sitting among other newcomers at
the introductory meditation group we had just started.

John Main had the gift of communicating in a direct and simple way the spiritual essence of the faith that he lived and served.
He saw the difference between the essential and the secondary
aspects of tradition. Seeing this enabled him to speak of it in a
way that connected directly with people who were adrift from the
meaning of their own experience but also in search of a spiritual
path through life. He was in fact a deeply religious person, but
what most people saw and felt was the spiritual in him. For many
this sparked in them a new approach to the religious roots they
had rejected. For others, he provided a theology of meditation as
well as a sense of coming home to the neglected contemplative
dimension of their faith.

Continuously re-grounded in his own depth through the daily
practice of meditation he was able to help others find and explore
the same depth in themselves. Others have this gift too, of course.
Such people are the real spiritual teachers of any religious tradition and each has his or her own unique voice and wavelength on
which they operate. Holiness, which is what their authority arises
from, is seen in them to be more than a moral or imitative quality. It is the embracing of their own uniqueness, a work that in
most cases involves a radical and dangerous experiment in their
relationship with the institution. No one breaks through into the
energy of the spirit just by doing what is expected of them or by
what ensures security and immediate approval.

What gave John Main his balance, clarity and depth throughout his journey was meditation. This was also what he taught with full conviction. He did not embellish the teaching with excessive descriptions of his own experience, but in his words, both spoken and written, people sensed an authority arising from direct knowledge. He has introduced countless individuals and groups to meditation, recommending a simple method he found in the teachings of the early Christian desert. To this day his simple, direct yet evocative teaching opens the door to many who are seeking this path.

If only a book could do it all. John Main cautioned people against reading too much about meditation. His emphasis was always on practice and, what's more, a daily practice. The weekly meditation group that he encouraged has become a powerful means of sustaining the practice, especially in the first stages of learning the discipline; it remains a foundation stone of the community he inspired. Through his original vision of the combination of personal daily practice and community, John Main's influence has spread far beyond the institutional church or religion itself in an organizational sense. It is a simple enough vision but one that has, as Raimundo Pannikar said of John Main himself, the 'simplicity of genius'.

The contributors to this book help us to understand why the influence of his vision has expanded so deeply and widely over the last 25 years. In understanding it we may better understand the signs and demands of the times we live in. Religious faith has a part in negotiating our way through the convoluted crises of the economic, social, political, psychological and ecological spheres of our lives. News of the imminent demise of religion was clearly exaggerated. A recent estimate says that a mere 3 per cent of the world is atheist. Even in Britain most people say they 'believe in God'. But religious belief alone is not the answer, as Jesus took pains to teach.

Religious institutions can serve spiritual and humanitarian causes with inspiring courage and dedication. But in so far as they are institutions, similar to those in education or business, they can be hijacked by egotism, either in their collective persona or through strong individual leaders. Power is deeply seductive even (perhaps especially) to religious people, and there is also a need in the psyche to submit to power. Without living contact with its spiritual core, religions tend to fall into the temptations of power and, to the degree that the Church does so, a mirror-image (what St John called the antichrist) can begin to form. But how to avoid repeating this only too human pattern? Only by being reminded of the Master's call to the absolute renunciation of power in poverty of spirit.

John Main saw that meditation is the simple discipline of this poverty, demanding but rewarding, that can help modern people remain spiritually alive and even renew the tired religious language and structures that should serve the transmission of wisdom. But he also helped us realize the power of roots. The deepest revolutions arise from the breaking of old patterns of social dysfunction or oppression within the hearts and minds of the ordinary people. The way to disengage from the power game of the ego that creates these patterns in society is to introduce as many people as possible to the kind of prayer that deals with the ego directly and radically.

I recently visited Haiti, the poorest and most neglected country in the Western hemisphere. Its once proud independence and prosperity has been destroyed by corruption and exploitation. Speaking about meditation there to students and schoolchildren, nursing students and parishioners, I understood better than ever before why the work of John Main is so important for our time. To teach meditation is to help at least some people towards the self-knowledge and direct knowledge of God that releases a passion for justice as well as the energy of peace. John Main was not a politician but he has left us a spiritual teaching of profound relevance to our time. If practised, that teaching can form a new understanding of what politics is for and potentially a new wisdom to bring the kingdoms of this world a little closer to the Kingdom of God.

1

JOHN MAIN AND THE CHANGING RELIGIOUS CONSCIOUSNESS OF OUR TIME

Charles Taylor

John Main has meant a lot to me and I have learned a tremendous amount from him and from the movement he created over the years. A movement that I saw at the very beginning, of course, when it was very small in Montreal in the late 1970s and that has now expanded worldwide. It has been a very important part in forming my own thinking.

I'd like to look at how the whole position of religion and spirituality in human society has changed so tremendously over the last half century, particularly in Latin Christendom. By this I mean the West, but I think you could extrapolate some of these points beyond that. And in that context I'd like to explain why I think the kind of meditation and contemplative spirituality that John Main started us on has a tremendously important role to play.

First of all, looking back 500 years in our civilization in the West we see a very different religious life. We are aware of this because we know some of the history, but maybe we should bring out some of the features of it that may not have been focused on. Going back 500 years there was a religious life in which religion was everywhere: it was foundational for the whole society. The King couldn't be crowned without it, and all the villages had churches; every part of the year was welcomed and celebrated by a celebration in the church; and various organizations, like Guilds had chaplains; everyone had a religious life, so that religion penetrated everywhere, at every level. Part of what we call secularization has been moving away from this tradition, in which religion and spirituality had become one activity throughout many compartments of life. Today you can go through these compartments, like university, trade union or business without ever encountering religion or religious practice; it is segregated out.

Another very important feature of early society was that it possessed a very strong sense of the sacred, that is, the distinction of the sacred from the profane was very clearly marked. There were certain people, priests as against lay people, certain places, like churches as against other kinds of buildings, certain acts, like saying the Mass as against ploughing the fields. Certain times, such as the great feasts as against ordinary times, were marked out with the distinction of the sacred time and the profane. Our modern word 'secular' was used back then as part of a binary between the secular and the sacred. Now this has fundamentally changed, although one consequence of this didn't disappear right away: being a Christian was inseparable from being a member of international Christendom under the Pope, Latin Christendom.

Once, being a member of society and being Christian were totally interwoven and, of course, the corollary of that was that there was tremendous pressure for conformity within civilized life, because being part of that civilization entailed being a Catholic. So there was something very wrong and unacceptable if you tried to belong without being religious (and Catholic). The first big shift began with the Reformation, but didn't really fully develop until a number of centuries later. And you can see part of it by the fact that being a Christian was being a member of Christendom, while being a Lutheran meant being a member of the Duchy of Saxony or the Kingdom of Sweden: it meant belonging to some quite particular Christian society. This was the first big shift. But a more important shift ensued with this rise of the nation state a bit later, where political societies were created by what I want to call 'mobilization'. That is, political societies began to see themselves not as continuing since 'time out of mind' within a certain law or constitution which people had always had, but they began to see themselves as societies created at a certain time because people came together to establish a constitution. Thus they founded a country that began running at that point in time, with a definite beginning and created by its human members.

And that is the understanding we all have of societies today. Every week or year we might hear of the foundation of a new constitution in a new republic resulting from new turnover in human history, and very often these new constitutions imitate each other. So we get this very modern understanding of society as created by its human members who are mobilized by certain ideas and certain principles in forming human society. You can see this flip over if you reflect that the early great turnovers that we think of as part of our history, the great revolutions, were carried out under the old mindset. Think of the English civil war in the 1640s, or the famous Glorious Revolution in England of 1688, which were carried out not on the understanding of establishing something totally new, but on the understanding of re-establishing something very old. They were fighting for the ancient constitution or for the rights of Englishmen or Britons. Even the American Revolution started off being fought for the rights of Englishmen that were already enshrined but had been abused and forgotten and somehow set aside by the present government in Westminster or George III.

It is interesting that the word 'revolution' as used in 1688 was employed in its original meaning: so revolution – the image – relates to the movement of the planets which move around but always come back to their original place. It is one of the ironies of history that we now think of revolution as the creation of something totally new. But the actual people who carried it out did

7

everything they could to make it appear in a different light. They called together a parliament exactly on the traditional system of representation. While they saw themselves as re-establishing the original, we now see them to be setting up something new.

I want to think about that new mindset and what it has meant for religious life, because society is based on this idea that we were mobilized, brought together to found a new society. We need a definition of what we're being mobilized around, what the point of this mobilization is. In fact we see in most modern societies that the point is very often a mixture of some kind of political principles (people may have set up a republic, for example), on the one hand, and some particular national or historical references, on the other (it is meant to be a Polish republic). The idea that society is organized around some central concept can also take a religious form with its sense of identity mobilized around religious principles or a particular confessional identity. In modern Poland, for example, the fight against Russian domination took the Catholic Church as a central rallying point. With Polish nationalism, too, the Poles setting up their own free republic were intimately linked with the sense of being Catholic.

Here, too, where being a Catholic and Polish are very closely linked you can see something like the original form of identity that we saw in the pre-modern period where being a member of society meant being Christian under the Pope. But there is a difference, because now identity is very differently understood in terms of how we create a society together around a central idea.

Another of the modern forms, and one we hear a lot of today, is the idea of a common religion being a source of, and the basis for, a very strong morality that underpins our whole civilization. We hear this from the religious Right in the United States, for instance, but more than that is the conviction that Christianity really means a very strong, definite moral sense and that this is what society (all of us) needs. This moral sense is, in fact, the only strong basis for a stable civilization. So once again our religious life is bound up with our collective life in society, but now through this idea of a very strong morality.

These modern forms reproduce the idea that my being a Christian *is* my being an American, a member of this society, or that my being a Catholic and a Pole are inseparable. Now, to complete this much too quick picture, we need to look at another tremendous cultural revolution in the West, which occurred in the second half of the twentieth century and which most people associate with the 1960s. It is much too simple, but it captures the idea to say that this revolution was mobilized by peoples' looking for their own authentic identity and beginning to search for it in all sorts of new ways. One of the consequences of this was that people also began to search for their religious identity. As a result, at a certain point, for many of these people a break occurred and their spiritual life disconnected itself from their belonging to the society. In other words, citizenship and religion began to separate off.

I think we have to see the meditation movement we belong to in The World Community as one of the fruits of that disconnection. We have now a movement of meditators which, in a certain way, readjusted its relation to and somewhat moved away from earlier religious forms in which this kind of activity used to be contained. Obviously it moved away from any kind of political or national framework, because The World Community for Christian Meditation is very much an international network, but it also moved away from the limitations of confessional boundaries. It is an ecumenical movement that spans different confessional boundaries, comprised of many different kinds of Christians united in the practice and teaching of meditation. If we look back to the predecessors of this kind of movement, the founders of the various orders of the Catholic Church, such as the Benedictines, we can see that they were exhibiting special modes of Christian discipleship but that they all saw themselves as contained within this larger Church. Now many of us do indeed still feel ourselves very much part of a larger Church but we live that sense of belonging through our common meditative life. The practice of meditation is foundational for the movement itself in its relation to the Church.

However, many of these former connections have not just altered but somehow broken apart completely for many people today. Is that a bad or a good thing? Well, it is a little bit of both, but I want particularly to look at the ways in which there are bad sides to this. There are good sides to this breaking apart and there are bad sides to some of the things that have been separated because we now have Christian life and spiritual life moving in different orbits which don't always agree. They can sometimes be moving in the orbit of a meditative discipline, opening up the individual to a new sense of belonging to the world; or they can move in the orbit of a more rigid religious identity that one walks into, assumes and possesses. This kind of religious identity may also be connected to a strong conviction that only one morality is right and it is the only one that will ensure a stable civilization.

I have been talking about the West, but if we look beyond this we can see that there are analogies, for example in modern Islamism as against Islam. Islamism is the movement founded on the idea that you can have a political movement of mobilization to change society according to a formula which, it is claimed, can be discovered in the Qur'an in the early life of the Prophet and his Companions. You see a political mobilization here to renew society, or to found a totally new society. Incidentally, proper Islamism was very contemptuous of much of Islamic history, founding a new society on basic principles and connecting this to a religious identity. We can look at other non-Christian cases, like the BJP in India, which have very clear analogies to this relation of religion and society, even though they also have quite specific expressions.

We can also see a similar idea in aspects of Islamism with the belief that a certain faith has the key to civilized order precisely because it has the right kind of moral structure. So we have very clear analogies to the experience of the West and Christendom in these other expressions of religious life in the Islamic tradition. Within these analogies we also find similar examples of the third kind of development I have described, in the deep spirituality which people are developing in their lives within particular networks or orders.

I want to look now at some of the dangers that are involved in these forms of religious life where religion becomes in part a marker of political identity in a state and when religion becomes seen as primarily valuable because it is a source of civilizational, stabilizing morality. In the first case, the very fact that religion becomes a marker of identity in a state somehow changes the centre of gravity for spiritual life because this spiritual life is now seen as being connected to a certain kind of national state, in competition with other states and other political forms, and demanding a certain kind of recognition of its dignity from these others who are often seen as denying that dignity.

So you get a very powerful concentration on issues like the famous Danish cartoons and the demonstrations against them. Religion can become satellitized, often in a subtle way, to nationalism and a sense of national glory and pride. Then there is a subtle kind of loss of the central point of spiritual life, a pulling away from it, in the very fact that religion is made so much the marker of a political culture. If I can look back to another example, which is very unfortunate and happening as we speak, the way in which Catholicism and being Polish are joined. This once drove a really magnificent, courageous resistance against Communism. But the present government there is turning that link into a very narrow understanding both of morality and of Polish identity, causing a kind of witch-hunt of people who are conceived not to be really part of that particular understanding.

If you look at the way in which religion can be seen as the basis of a civilizational morality, you can sometimes see a terribly narrow kind of moralism in which the whole issue of how the Church should be defined and of whether it should stay together or split is made to depend on narrowly conceived rules. Issues of sexual morality as you now see in the great Anglican Communion threaten to tear the Church apart over what is ultimately not a very important theological issue in the central understanding of Christian faith.

So there are dangers in these other kinds of modern modalities in which religion is linked together with a larger political or civilizational identity. Now we come to one of the central issues of this danger, which is the continuing recurrence of violence of the most terrifying kind in what we thought of as modern organized civilization. I am not just thinking of the Nazi holocaust, the gulag and the killing fields, but also what is now going on in various parts of Africa. It is senseless violence and it is not easy to understand why it is happening. But there is one aspect which we can understand and which explains why there has been a repeated re-enactment of some of the worst kinds of violence in human history with every supposed step forward. The Enlightenment thinkers were clear in their minds that a major source of violence was what they called fanatical religion. If you could get rid of that, human beings would step into a new era of peace.

Let's now talk about John Main and meditation. We need a certain kind of spirituality that can somehow free us from the violence of fanatical religion. One thing that is very good is what I call a politically unbound spirituality, because we are not likely to be sucked into the view that some particular culture is the bearer of progress and freedom. But more important, I think, is a kind of unhooking from pride in our own identity. If we can stand back from that pride in identity we can break what chains us to the illusion that *we* are the good and *they* are the evil. The wisdom of this change of mind is that we see ourselves as potentially part of the problem and not just part of the solution.

I think that a key feature of this kind of meditation, whether it is practised in this World Community or elsewhere in the modern world, is that it allows this kind of distance from an intense pride in our own identity. And indeed the lack of respect for the identity of others is often the source of a great deal of violence. Meditation has, hopefully, as one of its purposes and one of its results, to distance ourselves from that divisive pride, provided we don't start priding ourselves on the distancing, and can truly move into the silence of union.

Second, one of the ways in which we can hope to overcome this violence, having made that first step, is to move away from the caricature and misunderstanding of others. Consider the wave of mindless Islamophobia that is sweeping large parts of the West. It is not enough to make this a negative move by just saying 'we've probably got them wrong'; we have to be able, positively, to go deeper into a new kind of understanding of them. And here arises a big dilemma: we are not talking about an ecumenical understanding between different spiritualities. An easy move is to say that we are all the same, fundamentally we are all similar – all these spiritual movements have the same point – and there is some truth in this. But it is not the whole truth, because the puzzling thing is there are really very big differences. The ways in which we grow in a spirituality, the disciplines and the devotions are very different. So we need a deeply paradoxical stance which is hard to articulate, in which we can combine a powerful sense of embedding in the disciplines of our own spiritual tradition with an openness to and feeling of admiration for what we find in other spiritual traditions.

I don't think it fully adds up intellectually, but as a lived experience it can be understood and be very powerful. This is something that John Main helped to teach us, not because he was taught by a Hindu or because he made contact with the Dalai Lama or because The World Community for Christian Meditation carried on in this direction he set and further crossed these barriers. This new relationship to other faiths is an interesting phenomenon because it is not one in which, as often happens in ecumenical discussions within Christianity, we either talk ourselves into believing (or talk as if) there are no real differences. If we do that we never get to learn about each other, because we don't learn what really is specific to each other's faith, what is really quite *different* and where some of the most admirable things lie. Being able to live with this tension of accepting difference because you know that this is what the Spirit is moving you to do is one of the things that we in the modern world have learned from a small number of people, and John Main is one of those people.

Some of the issues and deviations that arise from these other forms of modern religion are tied in with civilizational morality and national identities. We can free ourselves from these and move beyond them through applying some of the things we have learned from John Main.

I would like to mention two other things that I think are important. Another way in which we get trapped into modernity, which is an aspect of modernity itself, is its intense concentration on the notion of progress, be it something very sudden and apocalyptic in a revolutionary sense or something gradual that unfolds stage by stage. Now we all tend to be caught up in the idea of progress, particularly those people who think they aren't and react against it.

If you think of how a Christian might fit himself or herself into the history of the whole Christian Church, something apart from 'progress' comes to mind. Perhaps we shouldn't think of our relationship to the past in terms of progress. We can recognize across the gaps of history something more extraordinary. We can learn and recognize that we are what we are through a constant conversation with the past. That's what John Main did. He didn't 'make progress' over the past but found what was necessary for modern Christian identity in the way he rediscovered the desert fathers and John Cassian.

So we live our Christian faith today partly with that inspiration:

we cannot be what people were like in the past, but we wouldn't be what we are without being in conversation with them. Again that's the paradox. This is also the secret of Vatican II. In recovering from the Church's rather mindless rejection of 'modernism', the theology of the Council went back to the roots of the Church and so rethought what it is to be twentieth-century modern. This is the ability to live with our Christian history in a way in which we are not trapped by any past or present limiting framework. We can therefore be in a conversation with people from very different eras and also bring these voices together in ways that can be very fruitful for our time. This is something else that we have as part of the tremendously precious legacy of John Main: how, above all, we fit into the modern world's spiritual traditions. How important it is that we carry on his work.

cf. Thomas Merton's opening essay in Wisdom of the Desert (last paragraph)

2

THE CONTEMPLATIVE
EXECUTIVE

Leading from the Heart

Peter Ng

In the last four years, I have been working on an anthology of John Main's teaching, which has now been published as *The Hunger for Depth and Meaning*.[1] The work has been enormously enriching for me in terms of understanding more deeply John Main's teaching on Christian meditation and connecting it with my own daily practice. In other words, to verify the teaching from my own experience.

Wisdom and transformation

I was particularly drawn to a talk which John Main gave probably shortly before his death. His voice was frail but he spoke with captivating intensity and urgency. There were three elements in that talk of particular significance to business executives and leaders. First, he described the knowledge that we come to in meditation as not just simply new additions to the memory bank, but the knowledge of wisdom, quoting from Paul's letter to the Ephesians:

> I pray that the God of our Lord Jesus Christ, the all-glorious Father, may give you the spiritual powers of wisdom and vision

by which there comes the knowledge of him. I pray that your inward eyes may be illumined so that you may know the hope to which he calls you. (Eph. 1.17–18)

Then he spoke about the transforming power of meditation, as a process whereby our minds are remade, relating it to Paul's letter to the Romans:

Therefore, my brothers, I implore you by God's mercy, to offer your very selves to him: a living sacrifice, dedicated and fit for his acceptance, the worship offered by mind and heart. Adapt yourselves no longer to the pattern of this present world, but let your minds be remade and your nature thus transformed. Then you will be able to discern the will of God, and to know the will of God, and to know what is good, acceptable and perfect. (Rom. 12.1–2)

What I found most engaging was the third element, which was the sheer practicality of how he described the way to that wisdom and transformation. He said:

This meditation, this pursuit of wisdom and love, must take place in an entirely ordinary, natural way. Meditation must be built into the ordinary fabric of everyday life. It is by being still, in a very simple child-like way, by paying attention.

And he advised, 'To be fit for the great task of life, we must learn to be faithful in humble tasks.' Then he went on to speak about the humble task of saying our word, our mantra.

In the twenty-first century, we face more obstacles than ever before in our quest to live our lives with meaning, depth, significance and purpose. The distractions and demands that characterize much of modern living are particularly evident in the life of the business executive.

Busyness and consumerism

The first challenge for the business executive embarking on the contemplative journey is to take a step away from the busyness of the business world. The unrelenting globalization of business requires more business travel, which strains family life. Managing an international business across multiple time zones is taxing on both the physical and mental capacities of more and more executives. And, of course, the advances of telecommunication and technology have produced electronic mail over the internet which keep many constantly on their toes. In the past, the home or vacation time provided much needed refuge from work and the office. But today the executive is hooked to the Blackberry. You can see this most vividly in how quickly the business traveller whips out this Blackberry device the moment a plane lands at an airport, anxious to find out what messages had been sent while he or she was in the air.

The other problem of a modern lifestyle is that we are all in thrall to consumption; both our own consumption and the consumption of people who buy the goods or services that we produce. We are all in some kind of a rat race. The consumerist lifestyle forces people to work too hard in order to fulfil their consumer ambitions. Even sports and hobbies, which are supposed to be antidotes to our busyness, can themselves be busy occupations. Instead of giving relief, they often add to our exhaustion.

John Main was well aware of the predicament of modern people. He said:

It's as though we are rushing through our lives, and in our hearts there is the flame of a candle. Because we are moving at such high speed, this essential interior flame is always on the point of going out. But when we sit down to meditate, when we become still, when we are not thinking in terms of our success or self-importance, of our own will, when we are just in the presence of the One who is, then the flame begins to burn brightly. We begin to understand ourselves and others in terms of light, warmth and love.

John Main also saw meditation as meeting the urgent need of modern people who live their lives at an incredibly shallow level and who desperately seek depth and meaning:

> None of us would meditate unless it had occurred to us that there is more to life than just being producers or consumers. All of us know that we can't find any enduring or ultimate meaning in just producing or consuming. So we seek ultimate meaning. And we come to meditation because an unerring instinct tells us that, just as we can't find any ultimate satisfaction in consuming or producing, so we cannot find ultimate meaning outside of ourselves. We have to begin with ourselves.

Personal experience

I first began to learn to meditate about 20 years ago. My wife, Patricia, and I were then quite contented at the level of material needs. Our standard of living well exceeded what we had expected in our youth. I was doing well in my career and enjoying greatly the job of investing money. Family life was happy. We had two children then who were entering their teenage years. Patricia had quit her job five years earlier to spend more time with them, and she felt more fulfilled in caring for them than at her job. Yet there was for both of us a restlessness amid the material contentment. We felt strongly that there was more to life than material comfort and career satisfaction. In a kind of midlife crisis, we were searching for a spiritual path that could bring more meaning into our lives.

In hindsight, I discovered Christian meditation at that critical juncture of my life. At that point, the more likely direction of my career would have been an acceleration of the pace, to try to get to the top faster. Whether I succeeded in my career goal is now hypothetical, of course. But I feel sure that I would have paid a heavy price in terms of family welfare, personal relationships, health and spiritual development. Meditation put me on the road less travelled. I changed to a different gear, which has made the journey thus far more fulfilling, has restored a balance in lifestyle, and brought greater depth and meaning.

The discipline of meditation was a necessary antidote to my busyness as a business executive. When I first began to meditate, it took me about two years to adjust my lifestyle and daily routine just to accommodate the two daily periods of meditation. But that adjustment process was a blessing as it made me realize that I had been wasting a fair amount of time in trivial pursuits or forms of addiction. For example, I used to spend long hours on some evenings playing the Chinese game of mah-jong with friends, sometimes into the early hours of the morning. At work, I spent an inordinate amount of time in business socializing. Much of it was unnecessary, in the sense my presence was not essential and it really made no difference to my business or to the hosts whether I attended those functions or not. By weaning myself away from those trivial activities, I not only found the time for the twice-daily periods of meditation, but also the space and time for worthwhile causes, in my case to serve our community as the national co-ordinator for Singapore, and also in Medio Media and as a trustee of WCCM. With the practice of meditation, I have found a new perspective of time and how to use it wisely. I now guard carefully my leisure hours, and have learned how to say 'no' to unimportant demands on my time, giving priority to relationships. I don't think I have become antisocial; I enjoy my regular games of tennis and golf with friends and business associates, but try to limit the hours spent on them. With the practice of meditation, I have come to value silence and solitude more, and this requires a certain distancing from noise and crowds, and some abstinence from television and other distractions.

From my own experience, it can truly be said that in giving time to meditation, we are not losing but in fact gaining time. This gain is not only at the profound level of personal transformation, which considerably enhances the quality of our life and our work, but also at the mundane level in the sense that meditation will lead you to shed certain lifestyle habits that waste time.

As a frequent business traveller, I have also found meditation very helpful in mitigating jet-lag. I can rest better and sleep well even at odd hours. When we are far away from home in a distant country in a totally different time zone, there is an inevitable dislocation to our regular pattern and routine of life and work. The morning and evening meditation, regardless of where we are, provides a certain stability and anchor that mitigates the dislocation of travel.

A new level of consciousness

We all have our own story of how meditation came into our life at a certain point, and made a difference to our life. That difference is a new way of seeing life, of living life.

I recently read an inspiring book, entitled *Chasing Daylight*,[2] by the former CEO of the accounting firm KPMG, Eugene O'Kelly. In May 2005, O'Kelly stepped into his doctor's office with a full business calendar and a lifetime of plans on his mind. This was how he described his job:

This job of CEO was incredibly privileged, but it was tough, relentless, full of pressure. My calendar was perpetually extended out over the next 18 months. I was always moving at 100 miles per hour. I worked all the time. I worked weekends. I worked late into many nights. I missed every school function for my younger daughter. For the first ten years of my marriage, my wife and I rarely went on vacation. Before this sounds like complaining, I must be honest. As long as I believed I could handle such a high pressure position, I wanted it. I was profoundly devoted to and love my family. But I could not have settled for a lesser job. People don't walk into the top spot. They are driven.

That day in the doctor's office, O'Kelly was told that he had brain cancer, with less than 100 days to live. From that moment, he dropped his job and set about living his remaining days focusing on what was really important, his family, relinking with friends, restoring relationships, and preparing to die well. Before he died, he wrote the following words:

I had long believed that a successful business person could, if so inclined, live a spiritual life. And to do so it wasn't necessary to quit the boardroom, chuck it all and live in an ashram, as if only a physical departure that dramatic would confirm a depth of feeling about larger issues, including one's soul.

After my diagnosis, I still believed that. But I also discovered depths to which a business person rarely goes. I learned how worthwhile it was to visit there, and sooner rather than later, because it may bring one greater success as a business person and human being. You can call what I went through a spiritual journey, a journey of the soul. A journey that allowed me to experience what was there all along but had been hidden, thanks to the distractions of the world.

O'Kelly said he learned in the 100 days before he died:

- about enjoying each moment so much that time seems actually to slow down;
- about clarity and simplicity;
- about spontaneity and the need to rekindle it in our lives;
- about spending time thinking about our death and preparing for it.

I could not tell from the book whether O'Kelly had a practice of meditation, but it was evident in those words that he had moved into a level of contemplative consciousness.

O'Kelly stepped off the treadmill of a busy life because of his imminent death. He wished he had stepped off earlier. John Main saw that consumerism could lead to a dehumanizing of modern life, and viewed meditation as a way of breaking out of that pattern. John Main said:

> It is so easy for us to become dehumanised, to become just consumers in a materialistic, commercial society. It is so easy to live our lives in some sort of mechanical way, going through routines each day, but losing the sense of freshness, of creativity, of freedom. As a result, we live our lives in a sort of rush, one routine following the next, distracted perhaps for a bit by entertainment, by pleasure, or deadened by the pressure of work or play. To break out of this cycle, each one of us must learn to stop the rush of activity. We must learn the priority of being. We must learn to be still. That's what our regular times of meditation are about.

From my experience, even if we find the work of meditation, of paying attention, of saying the mantra a constant struggle, because of the unavoidable distractions, the discipline of taking time out every morning and evening will bear much fruit. Because of that discipline, we learn to establish the right priorities, and to distinguish between what is important and what is unnecessary. This will benefit not only our own lives and our families; it will also make a big positive experience to the life of our colleagues and subordinates. We will respect their need for life balance by not making unreasonable demands on their time.

John Main had a humorous way of saying why busy people should meditate: so that they do not become busy-bodies.

To meditate requires an act of faith. But beginning in faith will lead us to an experience that validates that faith. And the experience is that a contemplative practice built into the everyday life of a business person will result in a better business person and a more fulfilled human being. In the words of St Bernard, we need to attend to the business of businesses, and our first business as human beings is to allow the work of God to be done in us.

Five attributes of leadership

I would now like to consider how John Main's teaching on meditation can affect the practice of leadership at the level of business organizations.

To begin, it might be useful to take note of what the literature on organizational leadership has to say about the essential qualities of a good leader. The literature on leadership is abundant with theory, case studies, commentaries and personal models as recorded by many leaders in their memoirs.

About 25 years ago, I had the enriching experience of attending several seminars on organizational management led by Professor Moneim El-Meligi of Rutgers University. Moneim travelled extensively in the United States and in Asia giving seminars to thousands of executives and leaders in both the public and private sectors. He identified five attributes of leadership which in his view transcend cultures. These five universal attributes are as follows.

The first attribute is 'the will to lead'. This refers to a commitment of the whole person to a goal that is both realistic and worthwhile. Such an act mobilizes energies of vast power. It is a movement into the world, but it springs from one's inner world. It implies a readiness to assume responsibility for others, a willingness to exercise the authority invested in the leadership role, and acceptance of accountability. The will to lead assumes personal integrity. When 'the will to lead' degenerates, the leader operates from an egocentric need, to get others to do things that one decides are worth doing, for the purpose of self-glorification, self-enrichment, or for intimacy. Thomas More wrote that a tyrant 'is a man who allows his people no freedom, who is puffed up by pride, driven by the lust for power, impelled by greed, provoked by thirst for fame'.

Moneim describes the second attribute as 'clarity'. Clarity of mind is not to be confused with intelligence. Something more than IQ is required. This something is sound judgement. The most important component in judgement is emotional awareness and emotional control. Clarity is not commensurate to the volume of knowledge. In fact, too much knowledge causes overload and confusion. What is really needed is relevant information. Long preoccupation with, and interest in, an issue precedes what appears to be a sudden insight. What the leader needs is the ability, and indeed the courage, to simplify rather than accumulate knowledge beyond what is needed. I have had the privilege in my career to observe at close range one such leader. He is Lee Kuan Yew, the founding father of modern Singapore. Lee Kuan Yew stepped down as Prime Minister in 1992 but continues to serve in the Cabinet as Minister Mentor. One of his great assets is that clarity of mind which enables him to simplify the complicated. He has a particular gift for reducing abstruse problems to the basic and communicable essentials. He sees that every problem has a heart. If you can penetrate to the very heart, the resolution of the problem will present no difficulty. Having found the essence, he will define it to himself and so to others in crisp, brief and unusually simple terms.

On a day-to-day basis, clarity can be viewed as a habit of posing a simple question, 'Am I clear?' Going into a meeting, for example, you would ask yourself, 'What is my role?', 'What am I expected to offer?' or 'What can I contribute?' A supreme indicator of a leader's clarity is admission of uncertainty or of ignorance, 'I don't know, therefore I must find out.'

The third attribute of leadership is described as 'the ability to learn'. The ability to learn presupposes the willingness to learn. Some leaders stop learning when they reach a certain level of overconfidence engendered by success or the admiration or flattery from others. A leader may reach the point of believing that she knows it all. Obsolescence then sets in, along with decline of expertise. The leader must learn from her experience. And so the most effective source of learning is in the errors the leader makes. Therefore, learning is inhibited by the fear of making errors, or worse still, the denial of errors. Self-knowledge, or true humility, is the mechanism that makes it possible for us to learn. The ability to learn enables the leader to expand her perception beyond past positions and to adapt to changing circumstances.

Moneim described the fourth attribute of leadership as 'similar and yet different'. To be a leader, you must be similar enough to your followers so that they can identify with you, or at least to be able to make sense of your behaviour and conduct. Also, a leader must share or at least respect the core values and cherished aspirations of the group. But then to lead, the leader has to be different? His responsibility extends beyond the group because he has to regulate the interaction with other groups within the same organization or outside. To fulfil the boundary role, the leader has to integrate two opposing perspectives, inward and outward. The leader also has to interpret the organizational mission to the rank and file. Above all, the leader has to offer people alternatives to what they want. There comes the time when the leader has to risk making hard decisions that are not popular but necessary for group progress. In other words, the leader should be an agent of change and continuity.

The fifth attribute of leadership identified by Professor Moneim is abundant energy resources. He has two interesting insights. First, he sees leadership as a reciprocal flow of energy from one human person (the leader) to another (the follower). Second, he stresses the wise deployment of energy, which refers to the regulation of one's energy, the economy of energy, the direction of energy, and the impact of the dynamic leader on the energies of the followers. This is in contrast to the American model of leadership that emphasizes dominance, aggressiveness and assertiveness. Leaders, especially those endowed with charisma, can arouse the enthusiasm of the followers, but may ultimately have a draining effect on them. An overactive leader may waste her own energy and the energy resources of the group.

So Professor Moneim reminds leaders that there is a world of difference between kinetic energy and potential energy. Kinetic energy, as we learn in high school physics, is energy in action or energy engaged in motion. Potential energy is energy at rest or not manifested in actual work. In other words, kinetic energy is energy that is being expended, while potential energy is stored energy or available energy. Wise leaders operate with the optimum deployment of energy, their own and their followers.

The interchange between potential and kinetic energy has a parallel in the balance between contemplation and action. We can think of meditation as a dynamic state of rest during which potential energy is conserved, to be released as kinetic energy in the action that flows from contemplation.

The five attributes of leadership – the will to lead, clarity, ability to learn, similar yet different, and energy resources – are in reality not separate but interact and interpenetrate in the act of leadership. When you ask a person how his boss communicates he will refer to the boss's enthusiasm or lethargy. He may also say that the boss, being enthusiastic, overloads him with information, leaving him without clarity about the central issue.

Humility

I like to supplement Professor Moneim's five attributes of leadership with observations from two other authoritative sources.

Peter Ng

One of the world's best-selling business books is *Good to Great* by the American Jim Collins.[3] Collins spent five years analysing nearly 1500 major companies. He found that good-to-great companies usually have CEOs who had a blend of 'extreme personal humility and intense professional will'. This flies against the common perception of a great CEO who is pictured as thrusting, overbearing, ruthless and insensitive.

I am particularly struck by the emphasis that Jim Collins places on humility. We shall return to this theme of humility when we reflect on the fruits of meditation in leadership.

Authenticity

Jack Welch, the former leader of General Electric Company, is perhaps the most celebrated leader in American corporate circles. He was asked what core qualities were truly essential to career advancement. He gave a litany of qualities: smart, curious, collaborative, the guts to make tough decisions, self-confidence and humility (a combination he described as maturity), a sixth sense of anticipating market changes. Having listed those qualities, he observed that most of these qualities have to be acquired, developed and refined. He then suggested that the crowning quality of leadership is already inside us, ready to be let out. He called this overarching quality the authenticity or the humanity of a leader, who we are in our soul.

To be authentic means to be genuine, to be true to ourselves. Authenticity implies a willingness to accept what we are. It means not only trusting our strengths, but also facing our weaknesses, and being patient with our imperfections. We might say it is what true humility is about.

If we are authentic, we inspire confidence in others. We are emphatic friends and good listeners. By paying attention to others, showing genuine concern, we help people cope with conflict and anxiety. We are at peace with ourselves and can therefore help others to feel good about themselves. It is authenticity that makes trust possible: the trust we put in ourselves permits us to have trust in others and to establish meaningful relationships. This trust in ourselves gives us the courage of our convictions in difficult situations, helping us to remain faithful to our values. We are not flags in the wind changing with any pressure that comes along.

The fruits of meditation in leadership

We have surveyed briefly some prerequisites or attributes of leadership. These attributes are the will to lead, clarity, ability to learn, similar but different, optimum use of energy, humility and authenticity. If we examine these qualities closely, we can find a common thread running through all of them. That common thread is the extent to which the leader has transcended his or her ego.

The root of the word 'humility' is the Latin word 'humus', which means soil or earth. In other words, to be down to earth, being realistic, honest and truthful, to avoid the temptation to act as if we are the divine centre of the universe.

It seems to me that the transcending of the ego manifested in true humility is the link between meditation and leadership. This is how John Main describes the essence of meditation:

It is learning to stand back and to allow God to come into the forefront of your life. So often in our experience, we find that we are the centre of the world. So many of us see reality revolving around us. We think quite naturally of situations and of people primarily in terms of 'how is this going to affect me?' Now that's all right as far as it goes. But if we really imagine that we are at the centre of the world, then we are never going to see any situation, or any person, or ourselves, as we really are. Because of course, we are not at the centre of the world.

29

God is at the centre. Now meditation is trying to take that step away from self-centredness to God-centredness. And the result is that we find our own place in the world. We find where we should be. We find our relationships in the right order – our relationships with one another, our relationship with creation, and our relationship with God. What we discover, and what is very important for each of us to discover, is that we do have an essential place in God's plan, each of us responding to the unique gift of our own creation.

For John Main, the movement from self-centredness to God-centredness happens because the practice of meditation is a central onslaught on the ego. We meditate so that we may be made entirely free of the domination of the ego.

It is because of the tyranny of the ego that we see a business world today where the standards of ethics and integrity have been severely undermined. Deceit and lies have destroyed major corporations such as Enron, Worldcom and Arthur Anderson. Virtue can no longer be taken for granted, and now has to be taught to executives. People are increasingly sickened by the narcissism, greed and other 'me first' contrivances of more and more CEOs. Much of the general public now believes that CEOs are in the game for their own personal gratification. The good of their employees, their customers, their communities, and even their shareholders are merely ancillary issues for them.

The root of the problem lies in character, which determines values and motivation. This is a crisis that cannot be fixed by public relations spin campaigns, or stronger government regulations and accounting rules. Morality cannot be legislated. Those whom we elevate or hire to become CEOs must possess the distinguishing qualities of great leaders: the ability to build trust, inspire dedicated followers, and make service to others their preeminent priority. In other words, the core values of CEOs should be examined just as closely as their drive, intellectual depth, financial acumen or track record. Competence needs to be buttressed by character.

There is a renewed quest in the business world for the ethical mind, a moral compass. We need leaders who by their own example can create an ethical environment where people aspire to do good work, work of high quality that matters to society, which enhances the lives of others, and is conducted in an ethical manner.

How can an ethical mind be cultivated? An ethical orientation obviously begins at home where children see the values that their parents live by; for example, whether they strive to make an honest living despite temptations. As they grow older, their teachers and peers have an enormous influence. At the workplace, they are exposed to business cultures, good or bad. Employees may or may not listen to what their leaders say, but they certainly watch carefully what their leaders and colleagues do. As young people go into business today, the temptation to skirt ethics is mounting. We live in a time of intense pressure on individuals and organizations to cut corners, pursue their own interests, and ignore the effect of their behaviour on others. If leaders and peers behave badly and get away with it, employees may feel emboldened to emulate them. On the other hand, leaders who demonstrate ethical behaviour, especially in spite of the temptations of the market, inspire their employees to do likewise. In the long run, the reputation of the organization is thus enhanced. Being ethical really means not fooling yourselves or others. The questions to pose are, 'Am I being a responsible worker or leader? If not, what can I do to become one?'

How does meditation help to cultivate the ethical mind? How does meditation help us to develop the spiritual instinct to do what is right? Listen to John Main:

The mantra is like the needle of a compass. It heads you always in the true direction you must follow, away from self into

God. And whichever way your ego may lead you, the compass is always faithful in the direction it points you. The mantra, if you say it with generosity, with faithfulness and with love, will always point you in the direction of God, and it is only in God that our true destiny can be revealed. In saying our mantra, in the daily return to the discipline, we gradually learn to look beyond ourselves. We learn to see with a vision that focuses itself ahead of us, in God. In that focusing of everything on God, everything in our life becomes aligned on God, and everything falls into its proper place. Our order of values is gradually changed. Instead of the value system being based on the ego, on personal success or self-promotion, self-preservation or similar limiting factors, our values system becomes aligned on God.

John Main spoke of the power of the mantra as loosening within us the roots of the ego that constantly leads us back into self-centredness and desire. This is because in our fidelity to the saying of the mantra, we learn to take the attention off ourselves.

John Main explains, too, why meditation has to be a gentle, gradual process:

We cannot vanquish the ego by force. That would itself be egotistical. We cannot use force because force would be a self-directed exercise of the will. The principle to bear in mind is this – we cannot possess ourselves but we can be ourselves. The ego is self-consciousness. To change this introverted image of self, to escape from self-obsession, we have to change the direction of our attention, of our consciousness. In other words, the only way to transcend the ego is to ignore it. No amount of self-analysis, self-pity or self-distraction, will overcome the ego. All of these would be much more likely to compound the egotistical state. Meditation, the recitation of the mantra, is the way of egolessness. It is the path to selfless attention.

The consequences of saying the mantra

The basic doctrine of John Main's teaching on meditation is, 'Say your mantra, and continue to say your mantra, and be content to say it.' Why is this so powerful? Fr Laurence Freeman has commented that:

> It is difficult to suggest how the saying of the mantra commits us to the progressive loss of self and to the ongoing experience of conversion in ordinary life ... Nonetheless, it is absolutely true that simply saying the mantra commits us to living out the consequences of saying the mantra ... We can't meditate everyday and continue to pursue a policy of deception, of self-interest, of revenge. However gradually, we must also begin to commit ourselves in daily life to truthfulness, to love, to God. This is why it is our spiritual life which transforms the world. As our moral integrity begins to develop, our actions will inevitably begin to change. And so the reality of the world we live in, the world of social, political or religious beings, begins to change as well.

The core of John Main's teaching, according to Fr Laurence Freeman is:

> We must first learn to be, and then we will know what to do. The power to do good, it is said, comes from being good. What we do is only changed deeply and permanently by what we are. This is a way of saying that Christ is simultaneously present in our hearts, in our worship, and in our world.

Let us conclude with the following words from John Main, which have greatly encouraged me in my struggle to come to wholeness:

> Each of us must understand the power source that is available to us by being in the presence of Jesus. All of us are sinners.

All of us are capable of sin and of the desire for sin. All of us have sinned and do sin. But what is of supreme importance for every one of us is that we come into the presence of Jesus, we are strengthened by him, and our egoism is deflated by the sheer beauty of his being. The journey is a journey away from self, away from egoism, away from selfishness, away from isolation. It is a journey into the infinite love of God. With some of us, the end of egoism requires a big struggle. Sometimes, we are carried more or less kicking and screaming into the kingdom of Heaven.

Notes

1 Peter Ng (ed.), *The Hunger for Depth and Meaning: Learning to Meditate with John Main*, Singapore, Medio Media International, 2007.

2 Eugene O'Kelly, *Chasing Daylight: How My Forthcoming Death Transformed My Life*, New York, McGraw-Hill Professional, 2006.

3 Jim Collins, *Good to Great: Why Some Companies Make the Leap ... and Others Don't*, New York, HarperBusiness, 2001.

3

HOLINESS

Its Mystical and Moral Meaning According to John Main

Brian V. Johnstone

What I offer here is an account of 'holiness' as presented in some of the writings of John Main. I will seek to explain this in terms of the discovery of the 'self'. I choose this term because of the centrality of that concept in our culture and because it is also a key to the interpretation of holiness in the thought of John Main. There is, however, a radical difference between the concentration on the self in our culture, and the notion of the self in John Main's reflections. In the latter, the characteristic emphasis is on 'unselfconsciousness.'[1] I suggest we could read that word more accurately as 'un-self'-consciousness. This implies a negative attitude to the self, understood in a certain way, hence the qualifier, 'un'. But, at the same time, it affirms the consciousness of self, understood in a different way. The self that is negated is the self-constituted self or the self-made self that is so important in the public discourse of today. The self that is affirmed is a self that is given and received. This self is experienced in terms of what John Main calls 'pure grace'.[2] Such grace, as Laurence Freeman has written, overrules karma.[3] By this I understand the train of events that seems to lock our lives into a fixed pattern that eliminates true freedom.

Thus, what I will suggest is that the experience of holiness is the experience of the self as given in grace. This is the mystical element of holiness. Such an experience of the reception of our self includes the reception of the capacity to give to others, so that they too may experience their self, as received, as given. This is the moral dimension of holiness.

As explained by John Main, the experience of the self is that which is discovered in the practice of meditation. In my explanation, I will therefore examine his teaching on this topic. This does not mean that meditation and the understanding of holiness that emerges from it has nothing to do with the rest of life. The argument is that the experience of receiving and the giving that flows from it establishes the basic pattern for our lives, the life we refer to as the moral life. In meditation we learn radically what it means to be receivers and givers or, as I would suggest, gifted-givers. This both gives us the possibility and sets the basic pattern for our daily living, guided by love, justice, humility and the other virtues.

I will now take up in more detail the theme I have already indicated, namely, the two basically different meanings of the 'self': one of which is to be rejected and the other affirmed. As we move from one form of the self to the other, we move towards holiness. In one collection of his recorded talks, John Main spoke of the 'self' in combination with several different words, some negative, some positive.[4] The negative notions he uses are in particular self-denial, self-rejection, self-promotion and self-obsession. The positive expressions are self-discovery and self-reception, with one other expression, the precise meaning of which we will need to explore in some particular detail: self-realization.

Self-denial

John Main took as his starting point, Mark 8.34: 'If any man would come after me, let him deny himself and take up his cross and follow me.' However, in place of 'deny' he used the phrase 'leave behind'. He was explaining meditation, of which an essential feature is to 'leave the self behind'. However, this 'denial' or 'leaving behind' of the self has a wider spiritual meaning in his writings and my purpose is to explain this. As John Main remarked, self-denial is something that our age would have great difficulty in accepting. Our culture stresses self-promotion, self-affirmation, self-realization. Self-denial is thus a strongly counter-cultural notion.

What does this word 'deny' mean? Max Zerwick SJ explains the meaning thus: 'I treat myself as an other (alien) whose concerns are despised for the sake of Christ.' This expression 'alien' or 'other' would seem to be a stronger sense than simply 'leaving behind' if we were to take this as meaning simply 'don't think about your self and your concerns'.[5] But this may not be what John Main meant by 'leaving behind'. I am going to suggest that he meant something more.

In his commentary on the Gospel of Mark, Francis Moloney explains the meaning of the text this way:

> The disciple is called to renounce himself, take up his cross, lose his life for Jesus and the Gospel, and never to be ashamed of Jesus and his words. As Jesus rejects the expected messianic glory and embraces the destiny of the suffering Son of Man, so must the disciple.[6]

So what does it mean to renounce 'self'? And, no less a difficult question, what is this 'self' anyway that we are supposed to leave behind? To renounce one's self here means to give up the concern for 'glory', for status and recognition. To be 'self' here then would seem to mean to be 'somebody', that is, one who has public social recognition and prestige. 'Self' does not seem to have the more subjective orientation that we would associate with the word now in our culture.

We probably do not expect to become famous, to become a 'somebody' in that sense. But neither do we expect to be actually crucified as was Jesus, and as were at least some of the disciples. So we need to do some thinking and interpreting if we are to work out how it would apply in the context of meditation, which is our concern here. There is another scriptural text in which the word 'self' occurs, which is a key to understanding Christian spirituality. This is the ancient Christian hymn in Paul's letter to the Philippians (2.6). Paul wrote:

> Have this mind among yourselves, which is yours in Christ Jesus, who though he was in the form of God, did not count equality with God a thing to be grasped. But emptied himself, taking the form of a servant, being born in the likeness of men. And being found in human form he humbled himself and became obedient unto death, even death on a cross. Therefore God has highly exalted him and bestowed on him the name which is above every name ...

The word for emptying here is the very well known word *kenosis*. Some Scripture scholars argue that this text suggests a parallel and contrast between Christ and Adam.[7] Thus, Adam, who was not God, tried to make himself God; Jesus who was indeed God, did not 'cling' on to being God. Adam tried to exalt himself, Jesus humbled himself. Adam disobeyed God, Jesus obeyed the Father. So when Jesus 'empties' himself, he does not empty himself of being God, but he sets aside the kind of will to dominate and control that is represented by Adam.

So again, the 'self' of which Jesus is emptied is a form of self-exaltation, domination and control. So we may interpret the requirement to deny oneself or to empty oneself as calling for us to give up any form of the will to dominate and control, and, to return to the first text, to give up striving to be a somebody. I am proposing these two texts as a key to how we might understand the 'denial of self' that is called for in meditation, as proposed by John Main.

We could recall the words John Main uses again. I suggest that they fall into distinct groups. The first is a blunt negative, 'self-rejection'. Then there is the set of words, denial of the self or leaving self behind. In his talk, John Main opposes these notions to self-promotion and self-obsession. These are notions that our contemporary culture seems to foster energetically. In contrast to these clearly negative elements, there are some that are ambiguous, for example, self-affirmation and self-realization. Does the injunction to deny our selves require us also to renounce these? Is it really a requirement of genuine spirituality to renounce these attitudes?

What does it mean to be a 'self'?

In order to help our reflections here, I suggest that it may be helpful to clarify what it means to be a 'self'. The concept of 'self' has its home in the kind of philosophy that begins with the 'subject', namely that following on the French philosopher René Descartes, who had a profound influence on modern thinking. This kind of philosophical thinking has been very severely criticized in recent times, especially by those thinkers who deal with 'postmodernism'. They are reacting against and rejecting a notion of the self as 'self-constituting'. Some indeed would go so far as to claim that there is no 'self' at all. This would mean that the 'self' you are now is not the same self that you were a week ago when you taught in school, took your children to the park, went fishing, etc. So there are extended debates about what it means, if anything, to be a 'self'.

To understand more fully these rather tortuous debates about the self, we would need to study the writings of Charles Taylor[8] and Jean-Luc Marion, among others.[9] In response to the modern notion of the self, the latter author has developed the idea of the self as a gift. John Main himself was well aware of the gift of the self. He writes: 'In meditation we learn that we are because God is. We learn that simply being is our greatest gift.'[10] He suggests that we think of meditation as '… accepting fully the gift of our continuous creation'.[11] The key to this new way of thinking of the self is the word 'gift'. I suggest that we might think of the 'self' as a gifted-giver. We receive our selves from others; in the first place, we have received our being as a gift from God who created us. Further, we have received the gift of our being from an act of love on the part of our parents. But having received ourselves as a gift from others, we become capable of giving ourselves to others. When I choose to become a 'self' I can choose to become a 'gifted-giver'. When I love 'myself' this is the self that I love: not the would-be dominating self, but the self who gives. Thus self-love is not closed in on the self; self-love is the love of a self who is open to others, both in receiving and giving. In the light of this simple idea of the self as a gifted-giver, we can return and examine the different expressions used by John Main.

We could pause here for a brief 'metaphysical' reflection. We cannot really give our 'selves'. We can give to another that which enables her or him to receive and give, that is, love. But we cannot give our 'selves', for the self who gives must remain as the agent of giving. The only kind of being who could give 'self' would be a being who is definable, if definable at all, as self-giving. Only God can give God's self, because only God is 'giving'. There is no distinction in God between God's self and God's giving, nor between God's 'is' and God's existential act, and God's giving. This statement is not merely a kind of verbal game; what it means is that when we experience the giving of ourselves, we experience, in that, the God who gives. Those who have had the opportunity to study the theology of the Trinity might recognize what I have just said as another way of expressing the statement that the 'economic Trinity', the divine self that we experience as giving our selves, is the 'immanent Trinity', the divine self; a divine self which we can define as 'giving', namely as the giving of the Father to the Son and of the Son to the Father, a giving which is the Spirit. That is why Thomas Aquinas could say that 'Gift' or giving is the proper name of the Spirit.[12]

The divine self-giving is accomplished historically in the 'missions' of the divine persons, as Thomas Aquinas would say, in particular, in the mission of the Son of God in the incarnation. This leads us to a consideration of Jesus and, in particular, to the humanity of Jesus. We cannot understand Christian holiness without reference to Jesus and his humanity, and this was a key element in John Main's theology. As interpreted by Laurence Freeman:

> John Main stressed the importance of the humanity of Jesus of Nazareth, who awakened to himself within the mortal limitations we all know. But in his awakening he heard himself spoken as the Word. He knew himself as the Son receiving and reciprocating (that is as giving in return) the Father's love. His human self-knowledge thus plunged him into divinity. And so his self-discovery has more than an individual significance. It is the 'single and all inclusive awakening': of human consciousness to its source in God. Jesus can be said, then, to 'share' his experience with us and to invite each of us to enter his experience of the Father as our experience.[13]

Jesus' consciousness of self is therefore a consciousness of receiving and giving. The consciousness of our own selves that we may be given in meditation is a communication in the human consciousness of Jesus, and likewise a consciousness of receiving and giving. We could note here again that the 'self' is never a 'self-constituting' self, it is always a self, founded on relationship, the relationship of receiving and giving.

Brian V. Johnstone

Self-rejection

Let us consider now John Main's term 'self-rejection'. On the specific, limited context of his discussion of meditation, John Main identifies this choice or attitude as that of those who, when presented with the invitation to meditate, respond by claiming, 'Oh, but I could not do that. That is for monks, nuns and religious. It is beyond me.' This is a rejection of the self. One chooses not to accept the invitation to a new possibility. It is a self put-down; it means I don't have that kind of spiritual ability. But it is also a rationalization for doing nothing. Since I am 'nothing much' I cannot really be expected to try. It is equivalent to saying, 'I choose not be a receiver and a giver.' It may seem a paradox, but it is difficult to be a 'receiver'. To be willing to receive means to give up, at least to some extent, a position of control. Sometimes, rather than give up control, we choose not to be open to receive.

This leads to a reconsideration of what we mean by the virtue of 'humility'. If, in effect, I say, 'I am not up to much; meditation is beyond me', this may seem like an expression of humility. But it is really an expression of my unwillingness to receive, namely to receive the gift from God that would enable me to enter into the way of meditation. The virtue of 'humility' is, then, not so much a habit of putting oneself down, but an openness to receive from another. It is a willingness to recognize that I am needy, but a placing of my neediness before an other who is prepared to give to me what I need, in this case the gift of being able to meditate. Humility is the virtue of receptivity.

Self-promotion

The next item to be considered is the attitude that favours words like 'self-promotion'. This is a version of the self that our contemporary culture would recognize and strongly support. However, for a believer who has read what Jesus had to say in the Gospel of Mark and what Paul has to say in his letter to the Philippians, this is clearly a form of domination. It is an exaltation of the self, a seeking of the kind of public 'glory' and prestige that the denial of self repudiates.

Apart from this, there are the countless preoccupations that flood our minds when we seek to meditate. St Teresa referred to these as 'wild horses'. John Main's instructor spoke of them as the 'tree full of monkeys'. Evagrius Ponticus, the desert father who influenced Cassian, wrote of the *logismoi* that invade the mind.[14] It is as though in our consciousness we live surrounded by mirrors, we are always checking our 'image' in particular because we want to look good to others.[15] But there are many others and many mirrors, so that our attention continually flickers from one to the other and we cannot locate our true self. These images are the product or projections of the many preoccupations that feed our dominating self. We want to look good to others so that we can dominate others and control the situation. These images will come. We cannot defeat them by force, this would be trying to defeat one form of domination by another form of domination. We can overcome them by bypassing them, that is, by simply saying the mantra.

Self-obsession

The next combination of words that John Main mentions is 'self-obsession'. This could be taken to mean being unduly pre-occupied with ourselves. But, if we take the word 'obsession' more seriously, it can open our minds to become aware of something more. Where 'self-rejection' means refusing to accept the possibility of being given the capacity to be a receiver-giver, a gifted-giver, self-obsession suggests a much more powerful force. A person can become, for example, obsessed with guilt from past failures. This can become of form of self-identity, it gives the person a strange, warped sense of self, but it is a sense of self. She or he could come to feel that without the guilt, they would be no one at all. Therefore, rather than slide into being a nothing, one holds onto guilt. Being unable to set aside the guilt from the past, such a person becomes severely cramped both in his or her capacity to receive and in the capacity to give to others. There can be good guilt, in the sense of an acutely sharp awareness of having damaged another, of having taken from them some of the gifts that they had received from God. This leads to a will to restore what was taken, by the giving of new gifts. But the guilt that one clings onto so as to have some sense of self, rather than a feeling of being nothing, is, at root, a form of self-preservation. It is not an authentic guilt, since it does not promote and sustain self-giving. This is what I suggest we might understand by self-obsession.

Self-realization

John Main also mentions 'self-realization'. This could well be linked with self-promotion, but the connection is not necessary. Main quotes Niebuhr as stating, 'There can be no self-realization' if self-realization is the conscious aim. This is a particular way of restating an ancient problem in moral doctrine and spirituality. 'Self-realization' could be interpreted as a translation of flourishing or fulfilment, and the question becomes, 'May I positively and directly seek my own flourishing?' Or, to translate this again, 'May I seek to find fulfilment or some sense of satisfaction in being a "good meditator"?' We are dealing with the old much discussed problem of the place of 'self-love' in Christian spirituality.

On a first level we can approach this problem through a discussion of one form of 'fulfilment', namely pleasure. In the context of a discussion of meditation, this would lead us to the question of whether it would be legitimate to meditate for the sake of the 'pleasure' that one experiences in meditating. The issue of pleasure has been a topic of discussion for centuries. The generally accepted conclusion has been that pleasure ought not to be sought for its own sake, as an 'end in itself'. However, pleasure may be positively accepted as the accompaniment of a good act. From a study of the writings on meditation and contemplation it is clear that these can lead to forms of pleasure or delight. In researching the history of meditation, I read of an ancient rule of the monks of the desert that included norms for the practice of meditation. It was forbidden to make any sound: no coughing, no sneezing, no clearing of the throat, no snoring. The only sound allowed was 'a spontaneous sigh of delight'. I also recall reading in a Jesuit review of spirituality that in the earlier days it was well known that the practice of meditation led to spiritual delight. There are documents recording the decision of superiors forbidding the members to spend so much time in the house enjoying the delights of prayer. Their Jesuit superior instructed them to get out and do some work.

Nevertheless, while the delight ought not to be the primary conscious aim of meditation, since meditation itself is a good act, we may enjoy the 'pleasure' it may sometimes bring. The pleasure or delight is not our object of purpose in meditating; that object or purpose is the meditating itself, with the union with God which is granted to those who meditate. Nevertheless, a feeling of spiritual 'pleasure' and 'delight' may accompany the meditation and it is quite legitimate positively to welcome that. Of course, there are some who seldom or never experience any such delight. This was the experience of Mother Teresa, recorded in the book *Come Be My Light*.[16]

The next theme is self-realization, or, we could also say, self-fulfilment or flourishing in a broader sense than 'pleasure' or 'delight'. Recall that John Main quotes Niebuhr as saying that self-fulfilment or self-realization will not be achieved if self-fulfilment is the conscious aim. The response would be a parallel to that which I have given in regard to pleasure. Is our object or purpose in meditating self-fulfilment? The answer would seem to be no. Self-fulfilment, or self-realization, follows on from the good act of meditating, and we can welcome and accept it. But it is not what we directly seek. We accept it as something that flows from or accompanies a good activity, which is what we directly and positively will. We do not meditate to fully realize ourselves or to achieve self-fulfilment.

To illustrate this point I return to a consideration of the act of gratuitous self-giving to another. The good act is the giving to the other: I am fulfilled in giving, in that by giving I become a giver. But I do not give to the other in order to become a giver and so attain my own fulfilment: I give to the other in order to give to the other. But what then is the character of the good act of meditation that is accompanied by self-fulfilment? John Main insists that meditation is not a self-centred closing in on the self. Although it might well seem like that to an observer. Father John insists that meditation is a *mediation*. This must mean that we, in meditating, mediate something to someone else. Others enter into the meditative action, but how? Clearly while we are meditating we are not helping the poor or working for justice or giving concrete gifts to others. I suggest the key to an explanation is again the notion of the self as a given giver, a receiver who receives in order to give. Meditation enters here on two levels.

Traditionally, spiritual writers made much of a distinction between acquired contemplation and contemplation in the full, proper sense. The first required activity, thinking, reflection, active praying. It was thought that only after a long apprenticeship in this kind of prayer, would the person be moved on to contemplation. The latter was thought of as essentially passive, namely the experience of God acting in and on the soul, without human activity. John Main, and also those who follow centring prayer, do not make these rigid distinctions.

For more 'traditional' writers on spirituality, acquired contemplation meant a form of prayer in which the one praying was active, that is, was conscious of 'working at it'. This meant reflecting on what they called 'truths' and praying by speaking words at least mentally, by making resolutions, etc. 'Infused' contemplation, on the other hand, meant an awareness of being united to God, where the praying subject was passive, that is, not acting, but being acted upon by God.

According to John Main's notion of meditation, there is an element of activity, namely the continuous saying of the mantra. The older spiritual writers would recognize this 'active' element; we are conscious of ourselves acting. On the other hand, there is a difference: they would require an active process of 'reflection' on truths. For John Main, there is not to be a conscious reflection on the meaning of the words 'Come Lord Jesus'; the mantra is simply to be repeated. For the older spiritual authors the transition to the essentially passive contemplation was to be expected only after a long period of the more active kind of meditation. Not all were in agreement with this. St Teresa believed that it was possible to experience contemplation in the full sense after a relatively short time. For John Main, it is anticipated that the experience of contemplation in this full sense may well occur after only a short time, even if the experience is only momentary.

Thus, I would suggest that in both the more traditional account and in that of John Main, there is a complex, interrelated experience of both activity and passivity, of acting and of being acted upon. The allocation of these experiences to particular times or periods is not an essential feature. Of course, the active kind of meditation, or the acquired contemplation, is itself a gift of God's grace, just as is the more passive kind. The only difference is the level of experience of the reality of grace, the one grace.

Self-discovery

At this point I want to introduce the notion of self-discovery. When we reflect on the experience of meditation/contemplation we discover our selves as both acting and being acted upon, but as capable of acting, only because we are being acted upon (by grace). We thus discover our selves as givers (who are active) because we are receivers (who are passive). In other words, we discover our selves as 'gifted-givers'.

In meditation/contemplation we discover who we are in this sense, gifted-givers, and we then positively choose to be that kind of 'self'. We make that choice because we discern that this kind of self is profoundly attractive. We see it as attractive because we know that this self is a gift, and that behind it is the ultimate giver, namely God, who is supremely attractive. We make a choice to be that kind of self, which means that we choose to become that kind of self, which we do first by being open to receive the gift of that self, and then by acting to realize that selfhood, which we do in giving to others. Thus, the mystical awareness of receiving and giving in prayer, of an 'inner' receiving and giving, is the source of our moral capacity to be receivers and givers in relation to others.

Self-reception

What I have just said would enable us to make sense of 'self-reception'. I do not make my self, I cannot be a 'self-made' man or woman. I receive my self as a gift, as has been explained. Even in acting to give to others, I am aware that I am receiving, namely receiving the gift of grace, which enables me to act and renders me the kind of self who can give to others. This notion of self is radically different from the idea of a 'self-constituting' self or the 'self-making' self that emerges from modern philosophy. When I have discovered my self as a self who has received in order to become a giver, I can choose to be such a self. This is our 'fundamental option'. This is, as it were, the first choice of the moral life, and it is from this that flow all our further actions of giving to others. That is why we can say that meditation is mediation. It mediates between our reception of the capacity to give, received from God, through our adoption of the capacity to give, to our giving to others.

Death and resurrection

For John Main, holiness is not merely a transformation of consciousness, it is a transformation of our selves through a participation in the death and resurrection of Jesus. As he writes, 'the Christian mystery can be penetrated only if we enter into the mystery of the death and resurrection'.[17] The resurrection indeed is central to his understanding of meditation itself and of the Christian life as a whole. We could recall that for Thomas Aquinas, the resurrection of Jesus is the cause both of our bodily resurrection at the consummation of history and of our present spiritual transformation, a process that Thomas Aquinas called the resurrection of the soul.[18] John Main interprets this transformation in terms of a transformation of consciousness. The abandoning of self-consciousness is the negative side of the positive gift of a sharing in the human self-consciousness of Jesus: by which we become one with him in death and resurrection and so become one with God.[19] That is the meaning of holiness. John Main quotes Catherine of Siena: 'My me is God: Nor do I know myself save in him.'[20]

Notes

1 John Main, *Essential Writings*, Selected with an Introduction by Laurence Freeman, Maryknoll, Orbis, 2006, p. 26.

2 Main, *Essential Writings*, p. 24.

3 Main, *Essential Writings*, p. 24.

4 John Main, *Twelve Talks for Meditators*, audio tapes, Medio Media, nd.

5 Max Zerwick SJ, *Analysis Philologica Novi Testamenti Graeci*, Rome, Pontifical Biblical Institute, 1960, p. 101.

6 Francis J. Moloney, *The Gospel of Mark: A Commentary*, Peabody MA, Hendrickson Publishers, 2002, p. 175.

7 James D. G. Dunn, *The Theology of Paul the Apostle*, Grand Rapids MI, Eerdmans, 1998, p. 282.

8 Charles Taylor, *Sources of the Self: The Making of the Modern Identity*, Cambridge MA, Harvard University Press, 1989.

Brian V. Johnstone

Jean-Luc Marion, *Being Given: Towards a Phenomenology of Givenness*, Stanford, Stanford University Press, 2002. On the modern notion of the self, see John Main, *Moment of Christ: The Path of Meditation*, New York: Continuum, 1984, p. 63.

Main, *Moment of Christ*, p. 27.

Main, *Moment of Christ*, p. 3.

Thomas Aquinas, *Summa Theologiae* I, q. 38, a. 2.

Main, *Essential Writings*, p. 60.

Simon Tugwell OP, *Ways of Perfection: An Exploration of Christian Spirituality*, Springfield IL, Templegate, 1985, p. 25.

Main, *Moment of Christ*, p. 50.

Mother Teresa, *Come Be My Light: The Private Writings of the 'Saint of Calcutta'*, ed. with a Commentary by Brian Kolodiejchuk MC, New York, Doubleday, 2007.

Main, *Essential Writings*, p. 76.

Summa Theologiae III, q. 57, a. 2.

Main, *Essential Writings*, p. 61.

Main, *Moment of Christ*, p. 55.

4

JOHN MAIN'S CONTRIBUTION TO CONTEMPLATIVE THEOLOGY

'In meditation we verify the truths of faith in our own experience'

Sarah Bachelard

> I pray that, according to the riches of his glory, he may grant that you may be strengthened in your inner being with power through his Spirit, and that Christ may dwell in your hearts through faith, as you are being rooted and grounded in love. I pray that you may have the power to comprehend, with all the saints, what is the breadth and length and height and depth, and to know the love of Christ that surpasses knowledge, so that you may be filled with all the fullness of God. (Eph. 3.16–19)

This is Paul, writing to those whom John Main would have called the ordinary men and women, the butchers and bakers, of Ephesus. If I had to sum up the animating drive behind John Main's teaching it would be in these words of Paul. Like Paul, he longs for each of us to realize (in both senses of that word) the enormity of the gift we have been given and the power and love of the life that it makes possible.

For John Main, if we really knew the truths of our faith with our whole beings, then we could not but be awestruck, humbled, wildly joyous and free. That so much Christian living and so much Christian theology is done *not* in that accent is a sign that we constantly struggle to know the truths we proclaim. John Main thought that the cost of *that*, for individuals and society, is the loss of contact with reality – fragmentation, alienation and shallowness; for the Church it is the loss of the power of God, 'as if', he says, 'a city without electricity was lighting its streets with candles while a great power source lay untapped in its midst'.[1] And John Main's teaching was that our way back to reality, our way back to the living experience of the meaning and depth and power of the truths of our faith, is the way of meditation.

I have been invited to write about John Main's contribution to theology, and I am conscious that that might seem to be a slightly suspect topic. Because there is no doubt, in John Main's teaching about meditation, of the priority he put upon practice over theory, upon praying over talking about praying. He worried about how easy it was for us to become so intoxicated with thinking about the spiritual journey, imagining ourselves making it and describing it in the exultant language of our biblical and theological tradition, that we forget actually to take the first step. He wrote:

> When you are saying the word you are not thinking your own thoughts. You are not analysing what is happening to you. You are letting go ... So, do not complicate your meditation. In my humble opinion, the less you read about meditation the better. The less you talk about meditation, the better. The real thing is to meditate.[2]

This might seem to be a definitive warning against spending time considering John Main's own teaching in theological terms. And yet, in other places, he also spoke of the necessity of speaking about meditation and about faith. He said:

> It is impossible to talk about meditation as it is impossible to talk about the Christian experience in any adequate terms. As one philosopher put it, 'As soon as we begin to speak of the mysteries of Christ, we hear the gates of heaven closing.' Yet we have to try to speak, though we speak only to bring people to silence … We have to find some way of trying to explain what the journey is and why the journey is so worthwhile and why it requires courage.[3]

So, it seems, we must speak even though we cannot speak; we must try to express in words what can finally be known only in silence. Here we encounter the paradoxes of a contemplative theology, in the tensions between word and silence, between understanding and encounter.

In my view, John Main's teaching is a profound contribution to theological understanding. It shifts our sense of what kind of truth the truths of faith are and what kind of experience the experience of faith is, and so what it means for us to come to know those truths of faith in our own experience. In what follows, I want to explore some of those shifts of understanding with you to see how they illuminate our own practice of meditation, our own spiritual pilgrimages. I am going to begin by saying something briefly about John Main's overall understanding of the relationship between theology and the lived experience of faith.

A living word

When I was growing up in the Anglican Church, I spent a lot of time trying to believe what I thought I was supposed to believe. I had somehow formed the impression that faith was essentially about believing in the truth of certain propositions, and if I could just make myself believe what was said, then somehow my life would be changed along the lines outlined by Paul. Of course, I wasn't sure what it would *mean* to believe those things, what *difference* it would make, but since I felt myself to be on the 'outside' of the rest of the church community who seemingly had all managed this feat of belief, I knew that my unbelief was the problem. I came to think that what I really needed was an experience that would prove to me that the things I found so hard to believe were really true. So, I hoped and prayed for a kind of 'zap' experience, a road to Damascus-like event that would make it all real for me, give me appropriately devotional feelings, and allow me really to belong to the community of faith. Strangely enough, no such experience was forthcoming! And so in my mid twenties I left the Church, having finally realized that even if I did give my assent to those propositions of faith, I could not see that having those pieces of mental furniture rather than any others would make any difference to my lived experience of life.

I think that this kind of experience, this kind of difficulty with faith, is what John Main was talking about when in *Word into Silence* he wrote about the disastrous consequences of the separation of mind and heart in human beings. He noted that the spiritual masters of the Orthodox Church had always emphasized the essential importance of what they call 'the prayer of the heart', because they understood the fundamental consequences of the fall in terms of this separation of heart and mind. John Main himself thought that 'this sense of inner division' pervades our Western self-understanding, and that the twentieth- (and, I think he would say, twenty-first-) century word for sin is 'alienation'. He wrote:

> The mind is our organ for truth; the heart our organ for love. But they cannot work independently of each other without filling us with a sense of failure, dishonesty, deep boredom or frenetic evasion of ourselves through busyness.[4]

In John Main's view, the great betrayal of much contemporary Western Christianity is that, far from working to heal that division, it had actually deepened and perpetuated it. On the one hand was a pious and emotive devotional practice, designed to stir up certain supposedly religious or spiritual feelings; on the other was a theology entirely of the 'head', divorced from the wellspring of any living experience of faith. Neither route, on its own, can lead us into the *reality* of the Christian mystery because that reality is fundamentally about the unity of all being in Christ. How can we encounter this reality, how can we live it, if our religious practice and understanding themselves operate to dissociate our minds from our hearts?

Of Christian theology in particular, John Main wrote that its major problem is that so much of it is focused on thoughts about God that are not derived from experience. The solution, he continued,

> is not to abolish theology, of course, but to infuse spiritual life-experience into it so as to make it again a living theology that is generated by more than just the function of reflections on other reflections … Modern Christianity needs a strong, contemplatively generated theology which can engage the intelligence with all the ideas, problems and movements of modern consciousness. It must be more than reprocessed God-talk, human posturings in front of the Infinite. It must be God speaking in and through human experience, which is grounded in prayer.[5]

In other words, John Main was calling for theological speaking about God that came in the first instance from the living encounter of the theologian with God. 'Any discussion about God', he said, 'has value to the degree that it is truly a revelation.' And he quotes Evagrius Ponticus, the fourth-century monk of the Egyptian desert, saying, 'If you are a theologian you truly pray, if you truly pray you are a theologian.'[6]

I think, as I said earlier, that this understanding of the essential connection between theology and prayer shifts our sense of what kind of experience authenticates theological speech and, relatedly, what kind of truth the truths of faith are. I am going to look at these issues in more depth shortly. Before I do that, however, I want briefly to say something about John Main's concern for the livingness of Christian theology in the context of the distinction that is now commonly made between spirituality and religion. My reason for doing that is that that distinction raises a question about whether spiritual experience even needs to be expressed theologically and in Christian terms. I think this concern needs to be addressed, if we are to appreciate the significance of John Main's call for 'a strong, contemplatively generated theology'.

Spiritual but not religious?

Just over two years ago a group of 'younger' meditators from the World Community met with Laurence Freeman in Los Angeles for a week's discussion. I was among that group, which was made up of meditators then aged 19 to 39, from the UK, Australia, the USA and China. The purpose of our meeting was to talk about how meditation in the Christian tradition could be communicated effectively to young adults. That led us to think about the needs of that generation to which meditation might be a response and the things that might block their hearing the teaching. Among many other things, we discovered a shared sense that we could more confidently speak to our peers about spirituality than religion, and that whereas meditation seemed potentially cool and relevant, Christianity was not.

According to the distinction that is drawn in contemporary sensibility between religion and spirituality, religion is about exclusion and dogma, about closed systems, about being right and making others wrong. It tends to fundamentalism, intolerance and institutionalism. Spirituality, on the other hand, is about inclusion and universalism, experience and authenticity rather than empty form, the living truth rather than the dead letter. On this kind of a view, meditation is attractive because it falls on the 'spirituality' side of the ledger and not the religion side. So far, so good. This is precisely the contemporary mood that John Main had picked up, when he wrote of the 'searching hunger' of the younger generation for authentic, personal knowledge of the truth.[7]

But then the question arises, how does theology fit into this distinction? Although John Main was critical of the second-hand nature of the dogma pronounced by much institutional Christianity, he nevertheless articulated the meaning of the practice of meditation in Christian terms and, as we have already heard, called for a renewal of contemplative theology. His experience, indeed, was that meditation has the capacity to revitalize the dry bones of theological doctrine. For many in the younger generation, however, who have no particular commitment to the specifically Christian expression of the spiritual pilgrimage, the question is not, how can the truths of faith be made to live again, but why is theological articulation of spiritual experience required at all?

In fact, on such a view, is not attempting to articulate the spiritual meaning of meditation in theological terms at best unnecessary and at worst potentially destructive or constricting of the universal experiential wisdom of humankind? From this perspective, it seems that the language of particular faith traditions, including Christianity, might be considered valid in so far as it is symbolic of or points to some deeper, universal truth, but is not fundamentally necessary in itself.

Although, as far as I know, John Main did not explicitly address this question, I think he would have been suspicious of that kind of generalizing universalism. There are two issues I want to bring out here. The first concerns the relationship between experience and language. Part of what lies behind the question I imagined is a concern that concepts take us away from first-hand experience, and that all we really need is to have the experience itself. One difficulty with this view is that experience is in part made what it is by the concepts available to us to appropriate it.

Simone Weil, the twentieth-century philosopher and mystic, gave a striking example of what it means not to have the concepts we need. Observing the experience of French factory workers in the 1930s, she noticed that they suffered not only from the terrible conditions in which they worked, but also from the deprivation of being unable to put the degradation they experienced 'into thoughts [they could] think'. They then suffered the further violation of having their experience, their suffering, wrongly 'translated'. In her view, trade unionists, the working-class movement and its politicians, described the workers' ills in the wrong language, the language of economic bargains and of unjust wages. It is as if, says Weil, 'the devil were bargaining for the soul of some poor wretch and someone, moved by pity, should step in and say to the devil: "It is a shame for you to bid so low; the commodity is worth at least twice as much".'[8] Weil is here pointing to the great good that may be done for those suffering inarticulately, even unconsciously, by finding the right words to express their experience, and conversely the great harm, the violation, that the wrong words may inflict.

Now, the context of our discussion is different, but I use this example to show the significance of the language that we have available to us to express what we take to be the deepest meaning of our experience. Without the right language, the factory workers that Weil knew lacked the means of making their own, of appropriating, the experience they were actually having. It seems to me that the struggles of the early Church over language and terminology, which to us can seem incredibly arcane and irrelevant, reflect precisely that understanding of the significance of language. How we *name* our experience of God fundamentally affects how we *know* God. This is a deep insight of the biblical tradition, stretching from Moses' concern to know the true name of God in Exodus (3.13) to the First Letter of John, which declares the good news heard from Christ that 'God is light in whom there is no darkness at all' (1 John 1.5). It is not that the experience is one thing, and the labelling is something more or less arbitrary and optional. Rather the concepts that are available to us determine to a large extent how deeply we can explore, be engaged by and changed by our experience itself. This suggests that theology, and concern about theological meaning, is by no means an optional extra in the spiritual life.

But this, then, brings us to the second issue which is how do we know that we have found the right language, the truest articulation of our experience? Particularly in a context, identified by the young meditators at Los Angeles, of acute awareness of the existence and validity of other faith traditions, how can we unproblematically articulate the meaning of the universal spiritual practice of meditation in specifically Christian terms?

Laurence Freeman has said that the meaning of any question depends on its context, and that we should make sure we have truly heard a question before we try to answer it.[9] This question, I think, could come from two very different places. It might be asked in a way that expresses a deep concern for integrity, for whether what we entrust our lives to is true or false. Such a concern is beautifully expressed by Simone Weil who, even after she had had an overwhelming experience of encountering Christ, said that she still 'half refused' not her love, but her 'intelligence'. For, she said:

> It seemed to me certain, and I still think so today, that one can never wrestle enough with God if one does so out of pure regard for the truth. Christ likes us to prefer truth to him because, before being Christ, he is truth. If one turns aside from him to go toward the truth, one will not go far before falling into his arms.[10]

If the question comes from that place, then it can only be answered in the practice of meditation itself, the practice of patient attention and waiting on God. The desert father, Abba Moses, said, 'Sit in your cell and your cell will teach you everything.'[11] John Main says, say your mantra. Do not analyse, do not worry about your experience. Say your mantra and your practice will lead you into all truth. This is the priority of practice over theory.

On the other hand, that question might come from a more abstract, theoretical place. There are different religious traditions in which we find different theological expressions of the meaning of our spiritual practice. How do I know in advance which is the right one? The subtext seems to be that until I have a good and rationally satisfying answer to the question, I'm not going to commit to any one path. If the question comes from that place, then it can easily become an excuse for refusing the risk of engagement. The Australian philosopher Raimond Gaita has shown the illegitimate conflation involved in recognizing the possibility of there being a universal experience or reality on the one hand, and the refusal of particular language for expressing or wrestling with that reality on the other. He wrote:

> Great plays, poems and novels often have what is appropriately called a universal meaning (or truth) but they are not, thereby, suitable for translation into Esperanto: they are – and my point is that it is not accidental that they are – translated from one natural language into another.[12]

It is very clear from John Main's grateful acknowledgement of his Hindu teacher and his references to Indian, Sufi and Buddhist writings, that his commitment to Christian faith and theology is not imperialist or triumphalist. It is not, according to him, that the spiritual reality encountered through the practice of meditation cannot legitimately be spoken about in non-Christian terms. But genuine encounter between different faith expressions of the meaning of the practice must go *through* the disciplines and understandings made available to us in particular traditions, in their concrete historical life.[13] Any possibility of genuine conversation and union between different faith traditions happens on the other side of the narrow gate: we cannot hold back from any particular commitment and then think we are in the place of union already.

When I started to meditate, what I loved about it was that I did not have to try to make myself believe anything. It was not about assenting to weird propositions, and I did not have to feel inadequate about a failure of either belief or zap-type experience. It was a practice, and all I had to do was to follow the practice. If the practice itself led me anywhere, that was fine – but that was not my problem. I found this teaching immensely freeing. But then, after a while, I began to want to explore the meaning of the practice. I wanted to understand my experience more deeply. At that time, still in self-imposed exile from the Christian tradition, I started exploring the conceptual resources of the Tibetan Buddhist tradition to try to make sense of my spiritual pilgrimage. I found myself in profoundly foreign territory. In no way do I mean by this that those resources are wrong or bad. I simply discovered for myself, as the Dalai Lama has said, that it is hard for us to make the journey when we are disconnected from our own spiritual roots. For many of us, John Main has provided a way back to our spiritual roots, a way back to being able to put what we experience into 'thoughts we can think'. Let us then turn to look in more depth at his contribution to contemplative theology.

In meditation we verify the truths of faith in our own experience

I said at the beginning that John Main identified the separation of our hearts from our minds as the fundamental division within each of us. This basic inner division is what keeps us from knowing our own wholeness, and keeps us separate from one another, from creation and from God. In theology, he thought, this separation leads to a theology entirely of the 'head', divorced from the wellspring of any living experience of faith. As you know, he believed that the way to reconnect our thought and speech about God with God's living reality was through the prayer of the heart, the practice of meditation. 'In meditation we verify the truths of faith in our own experience.'

One of the real difficulties in talking about the spiritual life, however, is that how we hear a teaching is affected by the extent to which our hearts and minds are in fact integrated. We hear the same words differently, depending upon the often unconscious background filters through which we hear them. Words which intend to express a liberating, life-giving reality can be filtered through our alienated consciousness and function simply to perpetuate it. Perhaps the clearest examples of this process can be seen in the way that the teachings of Jesus have often been distorted in our tradition by being heard through the moralistic lens of reward and punishment, rather than through the life-giving lens of transformation and wholeness.

Likewise, it is possible for us to hear John Main's teaching about the relationship between meditation and theology in such a way that the teaching is distorted. What kind of a claim is the claim that 'in meditation we verify the truths of faith in our own experience'? One way of thinking of it is in terms analogous to the Damascus road experience that I wished for years ago. 'Oh, after all, it is in *meditation* that you can have the kind of experience that verifies, or proves, the truths of faith.' I think that this way of understanding the claim leaves us stuck in just the kind of division between heart and mind that John Main wanted to free us from. It leaves us with an essentially propositional concept of the nature of the 'truths of faith' and with suspect and one-sided concepts of both experience and knowledge. In what follows, my aim is to distinguish between that understanding and the life-giving understanding to which I believe John Main was pointing us. In doing that, I hope to show something of John Main's contribution to contemplative theology. Accordingly, I am going to structure the second part of this chapter by looking in detail at the claim itself, beginning with the concept of experience.

Experience

What kind of experience might verify the truths of our faith? Well, spiritual experience, of course! And what exactly is that? And how does John Main's appeal to experience as the necessary ground of authentic spirituality relate to his consistent teaching that in the practice of our meditation we must not seek for experiences, or cultivate particular inner states or feelings? The difficulty is that the word 'spiritual' and the word 'experience' both bring with them significant baggage from the history of our tradition. We need to untangle some of this baggage, if we are properly to understand the nature of John Main's appeal to experience. I'll begin with the word 'spiritual'.

In the New Testament, the term 'spiritual' is connected to the spirit which is in Jesus and is the gift of the risen Lord to the community.[14] The 'spiritual' is what is under the influence of, or is a manifestation of, the Spirit of God. An important thing to notice here is that the spiritual person, according to both Pauline and later Christian writings, is not someone who turns away from material reality but rather someone in whom the Spirit of God dwells. That, in turn, means two things.

First, the spiritual is not some separate dimension of life. It is not that the believer has a 'spiritual life': rather, the believer's *life* is taken up, transfigured, reoriented by the work of the Spirit sent by the risen Christ. Second and relatedly, spirituality is connected with this active presence of God, which works to enable new possibilities for human fellowship and solidarity, and not primarily with extraordinary inner feelings or events.[15] That is, spirituality in the New Testament is concerned with the reorientation, the reconfiguration, of individual, material and communal life in accordance with the pattern of Christ and empowered by the Spirit. It is fundamentally relational and transformative. As the German theologian Jürgen Moltmann has put it, it is 'the experience of God in, with and beneath the experience of life'.[16]

The gradual shift in meaning of the term 'spiritual' began in the twelfth century, when it came to be used not so much as referring to the power of God animating Christian life, but as whatever pertains to the soul as contrasted with the body. 'This initiated a privatizing tendency in the history of Christianity. Spirituality came to refer to a highly refined state of the soul, with the focus on how one achieves such states of inner purity and exaltation.'[17] During the sixteenth and seventeenth centuries, the term 'spirituality' came to signify only the inner dispositions or the interior states of the soul, and a new focus developed on theorizing the individual's struggle for spiritual perfection.

This shift then had a significant effect on the understanding of the relationship between spirituality and theology. Whereas the term 'mystical theology' had formerly 'referred to the "knowledge" disclosed to Christians as they themselves are known and transformed by the unknowable God, now it comes to be used as a technical term for theoretical teaching about the soul's process of sanctification'.[18]

As for the term 'experience', it is as Moltmann has remarked one of the least explained concepts in theology.[19] For our purposes, however, a useful distinction is between experience possessed or acquired, and experience undergone or suffered. Moltmann has suggested that our modern Western concept of experience tends to focus one-sidedly on 'active' experiences, experiences that we possess, acquire or master. These are experiences that we can say we have *had*, which are closed or finished, and which are no longer present to us or are present only as something past, as memory.[20] It is this sense of experience that often seems to be assumed by those lists that go around on the internet – 30 things you should do before you are 30, or 50, or 70. This is life experience to be 'acquired' – seeing the Taj Mahal, climbing Mt Kilimanjaro, bungy jumping.

But, Moltmann says, there are also experiences that befall or happen to us, limit experiences that we do not master. Elemental experiences of life, love, grief and death might be for us events *in* the past, but they never *become* 'past'. They are continually present to us.[21] We live with these experiences – they become our companions. Moltmann says that these elemental or primary experiences 'happen to us', they overpower us 'without our intending it, unexpectedly and suddenly'.

> When something like this happens to us, the centre of the determining subject is not in us – in our consciousness or will: it is to be found in the event that 'befalls' us, and in its source. The person who experiences is changed in the process of experiencing. So although in German one talks about 'making' an experience, it is not I who 'make' the experience. It is the experience that 'makes' something of me. I perceive the external happening with my senses, and notice that it has brought about a change in my own self.[22]

So – we have here two roughly outlined concepts of spirituality and two concepts of experience. Spirituality may be understood, as in the New Testament, as the whole of life taken up into, reshaped by, the Spirit of God; or it may be understood, as from the twelfth century until fairly recently, as a specialized interior dimension of life, divorced from the material, communal and intellectual life in which it is embedded. Experience may be understood primarily in terms of discrete events and one-off occasions, things which one aims to have in order to make life and oneself more interesting; or it may be understood also in terms of the happening of life to us, that which makes and shapes us as much as we choose, make and shape it.

What kind of experience might verify the truths of our faith?

Well, spiritual experience, of course! When the concept of spirituality is understood in terms of extraordinary inner events and when the concept of experience is understood in terms of a finished possession, cultivated or acquired, then the concept of spiritual experience comes to mean the opposite of what, I think, John Main intended by his appeal to experience. It is the opposite of what he thought verifies the truths of faith, or authenticates our practice of meditation. It also has serious consequences for our understanding of the relationship between spirituality and theology.

For John Main what makes our faith living and what enables the theologian to speak 'first hand' of the truths of faith, is not in the first instance some private state of feeling, a 'zap' moment treasured in memory. He does not deny that such 'experiences' in the sense of one-off events can happen. But, he insists, they are not to be sought for themselves and, by themselves, they are proof of nothing – in fact, he says, they may be simply a sign of poor digestion. Rather, the spiritual experience he has in mind is that of the New Testament and the early Church. It is the experience of knowing oneself, in the *whole* of one's life, as in the process of *being* shaped by encounter with the Spirit of Christ.

How do we know ourselves to be truly caught up in that process? Because we notice, over time, that we have become more loving towards others, that we have become more patient or gentle with ourselves, that we have become more able to see things as if from Christ's point of view. We know ourselves as no longer trying to manage or cultivate our 'spiritual' lives, but as allowing ourselves to be more and more available in every dimension of our lives to encounter with the living God. John Main said:

> Our spiritual growth can never be seen as an *accumulation* of experiences, rather it is the *transcendence* of all experiences. What we so often call a memorable experience is first and foremost a memory. But in the eternal act of creation which is the life of the Trinitarian God everything is *now*.[23]

'In meditation we verify the truths of faith in our own experience.' The experience is one that befalls us as a reconfiguration of self, a coming to be centred in the Other. Moltmann has said: 'The experience of God is always a suffering of the God who is Other, and the experience of fundamental change in the relationship to that Other.'[24] It is not something that we have, but is rather our entry into a new pattern of growth. It is true that this means that one's inner, felt experience of life also changes, but that is a by-product of the experience rather than its purpose. Its purpose is encounter with the living God. It is out of that encounter that an authentic spirituality and an authentic contemplative theology will arise.

How do we make ourselves available for that encounter? John Main's answer is, 'in meditation'. Which brings me to the next part of my exegesis.

In meditation

What is the practice of meditation a practice of? One answer to that question is to describe the method of meditating. The practice of meditation is the practice (according to John Main's teaching) of saying your mantra from the beginning to the end of the meditation period, letting go of all thoughts, desires and words. A second answer to the question is to speak about what the practice leads us to. The practice of meditation leads us to silence and stillness. It leads us out of the closed boundaries of the ego and into the infinite otherness of God.

A third answer to the question, however, involves speaking about what we must consent to, if we are faithfully to perform the practice, if we are to become truly silent and available to God. What is the practice of meditation a practice of? It is, fundamentally, a practice of dying to self, of becoming poor in spirit, of becoming like little children, utterly simple and pure in heart. As John Main knew so well, it is our perennial temptation to romanticize even the starkest and simplest teachings. Nowhere is this temptation so great as in response to this teaching about leaving self behind. I want to say a little about this danger, because if we are to gain living access to the truths of faith, then this is the temptation that we must renounce.

Iris Murdoch, the English novelist and philosopher, wrote that the exposure of the soul to God condemns the selfish part of it, the ego, not to suffering, but to death.[25] She also wrote, however, of the manifold ways in which we refuse and avoid this exposure, indulging instead in fantasies of pseudo-death.[26] It is the definitive letting go, the sense that I will not be here to experience my own death, that is the terrifying thing. Giving up self-consciousness, giving up looking at ourselves having the experience of leaving ourselves behind, is the final terrifying movement of faith. It is very easy, in our practice of meditation, to avoid that movement – we are happy to suffer, we even think that as long as we are suffering we are making progress, but we will not consent to die. That is the illusion in which we can stay stuck for a very long time. John Main warned of it in his first book on meditation, saying:

It requires nerve to become really quiet. To learn just to say the mantra and turn away from all thought requires courage … [M]editation is the prayer of faith, because we have to leave ourselves behind before the Other appears and with no pre-packaged guarantee that He will appear. The essence of poverty consists in this risk of annihilation.[27]

He went on to say:

There comes a delicate moment in our progress when we begin to understand the totality of the commitment involved in self-surrendering prayer, when we see the total poverty involved in the mantra.[28]

This is the complete simplicity 'that demands not less than everything', but it is *this*, he says, that is the condition of encounter with the living presence of God within us.[29] This is the dying to which we are summoned, if we are to enter with our whole beings into the movement of death and resurrection which is the great axis of the Christian life.[30] It is not enough to think this movement, to imagine ourselves making it, or even to believe that this indeed is the ultimate axis of reality. We are invited to hand over our whole selves to that death of self-consciousness. Meditation is the means by which we hand ourselves over, and hold nothing back. John Main said:

> Now the challenge for us is not to reject the world nor to reject ourselves. The challenge is to learn to sacrifice. To sacrifice we offer something to God, and in the Jewish law it is the whole thing that was offered. It was called a holocaust. Nothing was kept back. Everything was given to God. That is what our meditation does to our life … That is why I stress to you so often the importance of saying your mantra from the beginning to the end of your time of meditation. No thought, no words, no imagination, no ideas … Now perhaps this is the greatest thing that we can do as conscious human beings – to offer our consciousness to God. In offering it we become fully conscious.[31]

I said earlier that one way of relating to the claim that 'in meditation we verify the truths of faith in our own experience' is to understand it as telling us how we can have the kind of one-off, extraordinary experience that would prove to each of us that God exists or that miracles happen or that Jesus really is risen from the dead. In discussing how to understand the concepts of spirituality and experience, I have already suggested that this is not what John Main meant by the claim. When we understand the practice of meditation as fundamentally a practice of dying to self, however, it becomes absolutely plain that this 'Damascus road' kind of understanding is radically mistaken. Meditation is not something we do in order to acquire a particular set of experiences. Rather, meditation is our pathway into surrendering the very self, the separate, self-conscious identity that looks for experiences to 'have' in the first place. Meditation is a radical opening into a new possibility for being – being given and received as gift, being centred in and wholly transparent to the life of God. And what that means, I think, is that how we understand the nature of the 'truths of faith' is itself radically altered.

Verifying the truths of faith

For John Main, the great truth of our faith is that the risen Christ dwells in our hearts and, to the extent that we open our consciousness to Christ's, we are led into the very life of God. Out of his own pilgrimage into the silence, on the other side of that complete surrender of self-consciousness, John Main testifies to an encounter with the person of Christ, with the mystery of the Trinity, which is personal and wholly loving. In this encounter we are made whole, we know our union with God, with one another and with the whole of creation.[32] This testimony remains just words, a report from a far country, until we come to know it for ourselves. And we 'know' it only in so far as we participate in it, in so far as our consciousness itself is in the process of being transformed. 'The knowledge of love', he writes, 'is only knowable in love's transformation.'[33] Or again, he says, 'the knowledge that God has created us to share in takes possession of us – in a way without our knowing it, yet the consciousness we gain is complete as the self-consciousness we lose could never be. We live no longer but Christ lives fully in us.'[34]

Here we approach the heart of John Main's contribution to contemplative theology. There are two things I want to draw out in particular. The first is to do with the relationship between the knowing subject and that which is known.

In human life, it is very often the case that how we come to know something has little intrinsic connection with what we know. If we are learning our times tables, for example, the method of learning (by rote and repetition) is different from what we end up knowing (arithmetic). If we are learning to understand the structure of cells, then *how* we come to understand (by looking through a microscope) has little intrinsic connection with *what* we find out by looking. The method, the means, is one thing, and what we understand or know is another.

The relationship between our practice of meditation and our coming to know the truths of our faith, on the other hand, is not one of means to external end. It is not that meditation just happens to be a method that works to get us to this knowledge of Christ. Rather, the reason that meditation leads us to the central truth of our faith is the basic congruity between what is known and how we come to know. Meditation is fundamentally the dynamic of dispossession, a dying to the ego self, that is the axis of Christ's life and hence the axis of our faith. Meditation is the way that takes us to the Way. It is not just an arbitrary connection, then, that the tradition teaches between the practice of meditation and the knowledge of Christ. It is our practice of meditation that enacts in our lives the truth to which it leads.

To put this another way, it is only by following the way of Christ in our own lives, only by letting our lives be lost, that we are able to receive his consciousness and know who he is. We know as we allow ourselves to be formed in his likeness, and we allow that by consenting to the poverty of the mantra. This, it seems to me, is the meaning of Christ's saying 'I am the way, the truth and the life. No one comes to the Father except through me' (John 14.6). It is not, as it is so often assumed to be, an exclusivist claim about Christian access to God; it is rather Jesus' understanding that the way to God is the way of dispossession, of handing over, of self-emptying love. We cannot know the Way who is Christ, without being on that way ourselves, and only this gives our theological speech authority and authenticity. John Main said that the Church 'can only proclaim what it is in the state of experiencing – or to put it slightly differently, it can only proclaim what *it is*'.[35] There is clearly, then, no question of us as disengaged knowing subjects attempting to grasp hold of the truths of faith as objects of knowledge. There is no possibility of theology as a purely academic discipline, disconnected from the life of prayer.

Now it is not new to theological understanding that we can know God only to the extent that we allow ourselves to be transformed by what we know. This is the consistent teaching of the classical theological tradition, although perhaps muted and neglected under the influence of scholasticism and the Enlightenment. But what is new in the teaching of John Main is that he has given us ordinary Christians access to walking that path of dispossession in our daily lives in the world. He has insisted that this teaching is not just for saints or professional contemplatives, but that it is for every single person called to follow Christ. As far as I understand it, he said, 'The invitation of Jesus is given to each of us to take up our cross, to follow him to Calvary and to join him in his sacrifice and to go through with him, into the infinite love of the Father.'[36] Each of us, in so far as we travel that path, becomes capable of authentic theological speech.

The second thing I want to draw out from John Main's teaching is what emerges about the nature of theological truth from this understanding of the relationship between what is known and how we know it. I mentioned earlier a time when I related to the truths of faith as propositions that I thought I was supposed to believe. That way of thinking about the 'truths of faith' encourages us to see them as separately verifiable objects of knowledge. On such a view, the claim that 'in meditation we verify the truths of faith in our own experience' appears to be a claim that what we experience in meditation provides evidence for the fixed and final truths of faith. But if what we know in meditation is the Christ who is the way of dispossession, then what we know is a God whom we cannot attempt to possess definitively in theological speech without falling into idolatry.

Let me try to explain that more clearly. We tend to relate to Christian dogma about God as if it is the final word, the final set of facts, about who God is. I have been suggesting that we cannot understand what our theological talk means, unless we are ourselves already in the process of being transformed by our encounter with God. But what that means is that the dogmatic 'truths' of our faith might better be understood not so much as strange kinds of 'facts', but as speech which attempts to express and open up the possibility of the kind of encounter that would authenticate them.[37] They are the concepts developed in a long tradition through which we are invited to appropriate, wrestle with and deepen our experience.

Christian dogma, the so-called 'truths of our faith', in other words, is speech that emerges out of the lived experience of encounter with the person of the risen Christ. If that is right, then the truthfulness of our dogmatic speech must accordingly be judged by whether it leads us into and faithfully reflects that same encounter. Of course, as Rowan Williams has noted, the Church is constantly trying to fix its dogma once for all, to secure for itself a faith which is not vulnerable to that encounter with Christ and the dying to self that is necessary to it. In doing so, however, 'it cuts itself off' from the source of its life and becomes imprisoned in its own self-understanding.[38] That is why, he goes on to say, that 'dogmatic language becomes empty and even destructive of faith when it is isolated from a lively and converting worship and a spirituality that is not afraid of silence and powerlessness'.[39]

The dogmatic truths of faith are ways of speaking which, like silence, point beyond themselves. They are capable of being rightly understood only as we know them with our lives, and rightly related to when we know them as essentially provisional, always open to judgement and never securely possessed. What that means is that our lives themselves become the verification of the truths of our faith. It is not just that in the practice of meditation we are led to experience the reality that brings the truths of our faith alive for us. It is also that *our* lives incarnate that which we proclaim: our lives themselves prove, to ourselves and to others, the truth of what we live by. There is no independent access to the truths of faith, and there can be no verification of them which is independent of the lives made possible in the faithful living out of Christ's call and promise.

John Main's great contribution to contemplative theology is to have opened up a way by which we might speak, not only in words but with our lives, about the truths of faith that have been handed on to us from apostolic times. It is to have opened for ordinary Christians a way of truly knowing, which is to say a way of being transformed by, what we proclaim.

Notes

1 John Main, *Community of Love*, New York, Continuum, 1999, p. 7.

2 John Main, *Moment of Christ: The Path of Meditation*, London, Darton, Longman & Todd, 1984, p. 97.

3 Main, *Moment of Christ*, pp. 13–14.

4 John Main, *Word into Silence*, London, Darton, Longman & Todd, 1980, Canterbury Press 2006, p. 14.

5 John Main, *The Way of Unknowing*, London, Darton, Longman & Todd, 1989, p. 115.

6 Main, *Word into Silence*, p. 47.

7 Main, *Community of Love*, p. 8.

8 Simone Weil, 'Human Personality', in *Simone Weil: An Anthology*, ed. Sian Miles, London, Virago Press, 1986, pp. 69–98, 80.

9 Laurence Freeman, *Jesus the Teacher Within*, New York, Continuum, 2000, pp. 33, 24.

10 Simone Weil, 'Spiritual Autobiography', in *Waiting on God*, trans. Emma Craufurd, New York, Harper & Row Publishers, 1951, p. 69.

11 Cited by Rowan Williams, *Silence and Honey Cakes: The Wisdom of the Desert*, Oxford, Lion Publishing, 2003, p. 82.

12 Raimond Gaita, *Good and Evil: An Absolute Conception*, London, Macmillan, 1991, p. 34.

13 Cf. Mark A. McIntosh, *Mystical Theology: The Integrity of Spirituality and Theology*, Oxford, Blackwell, 1998, p. 5.

14 In this section of the chapter, I am indebted to Mark McIntosh's discussion of this issue in *Mystical Theology*, pp. 6–7.

15 See McIntosh, *Mystical Theology*, pp. 6–7.

16 Jürgen Moltmann, *The Spirit of Life: A Universal Affirmation*, trans. Margaret Kohl, London, SCM Press, 1992, p. 18.

17 McIntosh, *Mystical Theology*, p. 7.

18 McIntosh, *Mystical Theology*, p. 8.

19 Moltmann, *The Spirit of Life*, p. 18.

20 Moltmann, *The Spirit of Life*, pp. 21–2.

21 Moltmann, *The Spirit of Life*, p. 20.

22 Moltmann, *The Spirit of Life*, pp. 22–3.

23 John Main, *The Present Christ: Further Steps in Meditation*, London: Darton, Longman & Todd, 1985, p. 108.

24 Moltmann, *The Spirit of Life*, p. 6.

25 Iris Murdoch, *The Sovereignty of Good*, London, Routledge, 1970, p. 104. Murdoch herself cites Simone Weil as the source of this remark.

26 Murdoch, *The Sovereignty of Good*, pp. 82–7.

27 Main, *Word into Silence*, p. 23.

28 Main, *Word into Silence*, p. 23.

29 Main, *Word into Silence*, p. 26.

30 Main, *Moment of Christ*, p. 15.

31 Main, *Moment of Christ*, pp. 113–14.

32 'We are at one with our creator and the uncovering of our own harmony serves to set up a resonance with the source of all harmony.' Main, *The Present Christ*, p. 17.

33 Main, *The Present Christ*, p. 22.

34 Main, *The Present Christ*, p. 19.

35 Main, *Community of Love*, p. 6.

36 Main, *Moment of Christ*, p. 114.

37 See Rowan Williams, 'Beginning with the Incarnation', in *On Christian Theology*, Oxford, Blackwell, 2000, p. 82.

38 Williams, 'Beginning with the Incarnation', p. 83.

39 Williams, 'Beginning with the Incarnation', p. 84.

5

JOHN MAIN: PROPHET FOR OUR TIME?

Yvon Théroux

I did not meet John Main when he was alive. I have therefore had to use the testimonies of those associated with him. His writings summarize, in condensed form, his essential teachings on contemplative prayer. There are, of course, other forms of prayer such as liturgical and vocal prayer, but meditation is a whole other teaching. John Main had the privilege of rehabilitating the ancient and perennial tradition of silent prayer, practised first of all by Jesus the Master himself, and then by the desert mothers and fathers of the early centuries. His works draw on teachings from the fifth-century monk John Cassian and other spiritual masters who have stood out in the history of Christianity up to his own personal experience with the Hindu monk Swami Satyananda, in Kuala Lumpur, Malaysia, in the last century. There are also numerous writings by his faithful successor Laurence Freeman. To this we would also have to add present-day testimonies of hundreds of people who rediscovered in the re-formulation of the Christian meditation for our time a direction for their life and meaningful spirituality. This is a great achievement. But, in what way can we say that John Main was a prophet for our time?

What does the word 'prophet' mean?

This is not an honorary title to flatter a man whose spiritual stature was greater than life. The term, 'prophet for our time', is not a post-mortem tribute. It is rather a very personal reading of the work and life of this man who was born in a family that had deep-rooted catholic religious convictions. What is meant by the word 'catholic' here is a universal openness to other human beings, no matter who they are in the absence of any form of discrimination. Let us specify that the term prophet comes from the Greek word *prophētēs*. Etymologically, this word does not designate one who foresees the future but 'one who speaks in the place of'. Even when he was still very young, John Main could distinguish aspects related to faith and those related to religion. Paul Harris, in his book *Christian Meditation by Those Who Practice It,*[1] refers to the resolutely free character of John Main's mother regarding certain religious principles of the time. Therefore, we must not be surprised to see an expression of inner freedom manifested in the writings of her son. He himself would like this universality to carry the seal of a dialogue of total respect for every human being regardless of their ethnic, cultural or religious background.

Baptism and prophetic function

John Main was baptized John Douglas Main. Baptism, the rite of Christian initiation in Christianity, breathes the life of the prophet into every person who receives it. Jesus himself was baptized by John in the Jordan (Mark 1.9–11). He was, in a way, the disciple of John the Baptist even before he himself baptized or asked others to baptize (John 4.1–2). Jesus will be seen above all as a *prophet,* even by Islam, which considers him as one of the main prophets along with Abraham, Moses and David. We are reminded of the baptism ritual at the very beginning of his public life, shortly before he set off on his spiritual adventure in his early thirties.

When I look at the life of John Main, who worked in London as a journalist, then joined the ranks of the Intelligence Service during World War II in England and Belgium, before joining the Regular Canons for a brief period of time and finally obtained a law diploma at Trinity College, I can see that this period of time in his life could not have been circumvented. He had to reach a certain maturity, after the time he was baptized, before committing himself in a mission that continues to bear fruit to this day. The important events that occur in our lives are the interpellations or questions God gives us to grow.

At the age of 28, he was in Malaysia as a diplomat in the British Foreign Service. At the age of 30, he became a law professor. Then, when the death of his young nephew turned his life upside down, he reflected seriously and entered the Benedictine Abbey of Ealing, in London. Nineteen years later, at the age of 49, John Main gathered his first community of meditators at his monastery. At the age of 51, he founded a priory in Montreal with a view to initiating people in Christian meditation. Five years later he died, leaving a then fragile but promising and fruitful legacy.

One has to mature before accomplishing a work that can be filled with the Spirit and prophetic vision. No one can accomplish an undertaking such as the one John Main accomplished without being called by Jesus who came to reveal his Father, author of all life. One cannot self-proclaim himself a prophet. Each one carries his or her own destiny with its lot of sufferings, sorrows, joys and consolations.

The times and the environment 'carve' the prophet

Prophets are influenced by the times in which they live and their native environments. This will, to some degree, influence the essential aspects of their message. John Douglas Main, the third child of David and Eileen Main, would have been influenced by Ballinskelligs, County Kerry and that environment. The working experience of his father and grandfather with the first telegraph station by transatlantic cable gave them an unparalleled sense of openness to the world. And the ancient Celtic monastic witness of the hermitages situated at the summit of Skellig Michael must have been particularly meaningful for John Main as he rediscovered contemplation.

Later on, it is of no surprise to see John Main become friends with Swami Satyananda, whom he considered a 'holy Hindu monk', a spiritual master guided by the Spirit because he was totally dedicated to the service of others. In this man's teaching on prayer John Main recognized the quality of the biblical prophet 'speaking on behalf of God'.

The prophet of Israel, Micah of Moresheth, who came from a poor population of country folk, was obliged to find refuge in Jerusalem. He was angered by the luxury he found there. Jesus came from Nazareth, a place that was not supposed to give such prophets. In the last century, John Main made a correct diagnosis of the spiritual poverty of his fellow Christians and the treasure of contemplation that had fallen into oblivion for so many centuries because it was not accessible to the people of God as a whole. From early times to this day, starting with Deborah, Ezekiel, Isaiah, Hosea, Amos and so many others, including John Cassian, Benedict, John of the Cross, Teresa of Avila, the author of the *Cloud of the Unknowing,* Augustine Baker, Thomas Merton, Jules Monchanin, Bede Griffiths and John Main, prophets were always influenced by their early beginnings and their intimate family life. They were incarnated in the here and now of their times, in the culture and in the spirituality of their own historical epoch.

Yvon Théroux

The unprecedented destiny of the prophets

Marked by the limits of humanity, these women and men had an extraordinary destiny. We can well imagine the sadness John Main experienced when, as a young novice with the Benedictines, he was forbidden to practise meditation as he had learned from his Hindu friend. He admitted that this was a period of great spiritual dryness for him. At other times, it was Amos who was expelled from the sanctuary of Bethel (Amos 7.10–17; 2.12). Jeremiah was also subject to hatred on the part of the officers and priests (Jer. 37.16–21). Jesus himself became embroiled in a political process and was betrayed. During his lifetime, John Main suffered opposition from certain people in his environment with regard to the practice and then the teaching of the mantra that he had used. There are many reasons for these misunderstandings. It is true for all times and generations that to proclaim and to teach contemplative prayer goes against the tide. It is not easy to invite women and men of our time to contact the Presence at the centre of their being. Allow me, here, to tell you of a legend from the Hindu tradition.

The Transcendence, let us say God, had to remain inaccessible to the common people. Two groups of wise men gathered to try to find what would be the best solution to hide God. The first time they met, one of the wise men suggested that God be hidden at the summit of the highest mountains. But one of the wise men said that one day the humans would reach the eternal summits and discover the 'All Powerful One'. After a long period of reflection, another wise man suggested another solution: 'Let us hide him in the depths of the ocean', but the wise men said that the humans would no doubt explore the depths of the ocean and discover the Mystery. Then, two groups of wise men got together and came up with this solution: 'Let us hide him in the human heart. People will never think of looking for God there', and of this they were absolutely convinced.

The proclamation of a message that is anti-conformist, and even goes against the mentality of the time is well tried. The proposal made by John Main to Christians at the end of the last century was a way of great simplicity and yet a way that is difficult in its daily practice because it consists of a discipline that includes body, spirit and heart. There is no substitute for the effort of entering within, into the deep silence of inner life where there are no words, no chattering and in the end no thoughts. There is only room to listen, to listen to God hidden in the depth of our being. John Main's destiny was to live and teach this.

John Main found himself among foreign populations, which had been conquered many years before by the British Empire. He later became headmaster of a school in Washington DC and finally, in the latter part of his life, he accepted the invitation of the English Auxiliary Bishop of Montreal, Leonard Crowley, to come and found a priory in Canada to teach Christian meditation. It was his 'fiat' in accepting this that led to a new form of monasticism and oblate communities centred on meditation. His answer was alive and life-giving for those who were sincerely seeking the way, the truth and the life. In the early history of Israel, the prophets were visionaries. Their horizon made room for an openness which would activate the best in human beings and stimulate their will to search for the best in themselves, which is the Presence, the silent Word that is the Word. Amos made reference to 'the people of Yahweh' who were seeking God (Amos 5.4–5). Isaiah's vision led him to understand that the people *see* God and in doing so they *know* God's plan for them (Isa. 6). John Main invited the people to contact this essential insight in their own hearts.

The gesture reinforces the prophetic word

More often than not the prophet reinforces the word by acts. The commitment of John Main was wholehearted; it wasn't lukewarm nor were there superficial compromises. His relationship with God is expressed in his teachings and in his contacts with individuals or groups. This God-centred awareness of the prophet evolved into a mission by which prophets spoke on behalf of God. The hesitations of the prophets of all times, their procrastinations, their moments of doubt, are all part of the journey. They found consolation and courage in the intimate relationship that had been established with God. In biblical terms, the evocative expression 'I am with you' is the fruit of a mutual presence. The prophet becomes a 'watcher', a 'guard', an 'awakener of conscience'. John Main, in his teaching of meditation, insists on the importance of remaining relaxed but vigilant when meditating. We have to retire within our self, to strive for inner unity. We are split, fragmented, scattered in all directions. When we are not occupied, we are preoccupied. Our sense of identity is bound to our actions and to our thoughts. John Main taught us a way to a deeper centre from which thought and action could find a new correspondence and harmony. All the realities of our being have to be unified by meditation. Contemplation has nothing to do with a purely external religiosity. It is the unification of one's being in relation with our self, with the cosmos and with others. We have to become attentive to reach this goal.

To be attentive does not mean just to reflect. It is the vigilant attitude of one's whole being tending towards the presence of the Reality within. This attitude of attention leads towards truth and the unity of being. If, as John Main says, we must not have any expectations when we meditate, we must nevertheless cultivate patience and perseverance. Attention is a power of inner transformation (*metanoia,* in Greek). There the Presence of God fully plays its role in an environment of an inspiring silence.

Silence is the music of the soul. Outer silence leads to inner silence. The author of Ecclesiastes teaches us that the more words, the greater the vanity of it all (Eccles. 6.11). The author also adds, 'Be in no hurry to speak' (Eccles. 5.1). This third highly spiritual attitude generates the need to listen.

Listen to the silence! Its murmuring reveals the One who dwells in our hearts as Paul once said to the Galatians: 'I live now not with my own life but with the life of Christ who lives in me' (Gal. 2.20). Learning to listen is rapture. It is absolutely necessary to become who we are and to get to know ourselves in depth. These attitudes give power to the prophetic word. The personal conviction that John Main wishes to share through the teachings of Christian meditation echoes an experience of faith lived with intensity. It radiates.

Prophets authentically manifest their certainty that the word which echoes comes from Someone greater than them. The Word of God literally dwells in them. The teachings and the writings of John Main bear witness to the fact that the Word dwells in him: numerous quotations are taken from the holy Scriptures. Like Jeremiah, John Main could have said, 'Your words are like fire burning in my heart, imprisoned in my bones' (Jer. 15.16). This total surrender to God's will, freely consented to, speaks of the prophet's new relationship with God, with the world, with others, an enriched relationship from which wise words and counsel emerge.

The close link between the prophet and the people of God

In the Hebrew Bible – the First Testament of Christian writings – those in charge of teaching catechism underlined the close link between the prophet and the people. All the prophets, from early times to this day, play an indispensable role at the level of lived faith. In this experience of lived faith, the tension of interiority and universalism is resolved in the activation of each one's conscience. Isaiah invites each one to respond to the invitation addressed to all people: that they turn towards the unique God who dwells in the heart of all humans. John Main sowed seeds of ecumenism and interreligious dialogue based on his own personal experience, both human and spiritual. There again, is this not the fruit of what he had learned in his childhood when his family welcomed 'orphaned children, single mothers, abandoned or alcoholic spouses ... They were not only welcomed into their household, but very often they were given the bedroom of a family member who then had to sleep on the sofa in the living room.'[2]

If people are influenced by their past, so are whole communities. Quebec, for example, has had a particular religious history rooted in Catholicism. This used to be part of the social fabric but now, in the face of a secular outlook, it has become a more distinct identity. With this concern to define itself comes the danger of institutionalization. At the present one could say that Catholicism is at death's door at the structural level. However there are signs of a new spring when we see the fervour of the Christian meditation communities that are striving to renew with the essential. There is a spiritual core at the heart of a faith that is stronger than religious structures. It is in this place of the meeting of interiority and openness that the five years John Main spent in the metropolis of Quebec is bearing fruit.

The prophetic tradition throughout the ages

The early Church had a few prophets, for example Barnaby (Acts 4.36), Agabus (Acts 11.28; 21.10–14), Jude and Silas (Acts 15.32). The community of Antioch was led by a team of prophets and catechetical teachers (Acts 13.1). Paul ranks among the prophets immediately after the Apostles.

By observing present times attentively, perhaps we will see in John Main, in Mother Teresa of Calcutta, or Jean Vanier prophets in the biblical sense. We should be aware of the outpouring of the prophetic charism (1 Cor. 14) present throughout the history of Christianity and of the Church.

Ireneus of Lyon was someone who saw the prophetic charism as one of the indelible marks of the Church. Part of the prophetic charism is to renew the Church by reminding us of sacred traditions, adopting new ways of seeing and living them, and adapting them for Christians in the contemporary world. It is in this daring perspective of openness to the world that John Main is situated and can be recognized as one who has the charism to speak on behalf of God. If we cast a quick look at the fruitful harvest of this prophetic seed, we see a huge number of meditation groups present in almost all the continents, and numerous individuals who meditate alone in union with the world community. John Main had a sense that his life would be rather short. This is probably the reason why he had ensured a replacement in Laurence Freeman. He wrote inspiring teachings because he was inspired. His teachings are filled with wisdom that gives serenity and joy, inner peace and tranquility, love of silence and communion with the One who dwells in our heart.

A work beyond measure by the prophet

When we read the quarterly bulletin of The World Community for Christian Meditation, we see the consequences of John Main's creative initiative. His teaching was not extinguished by his early death in 1982. The rapid growth of the meditation tree reminds us of the parable of the seed planted in good soil (Matt. 13.3–9). The numerous trips made by Laurence Freeman remind us of those made by Paul and his companions in the early Church. A form of Christianity is dying to allow *Christianity* to emerge. A return to the essentials; that is, a faithful attachment to Jesus who came to reveal the Father and who summarized the whole Law through love of self, others and God. The inner experience of this faith replaces the rituals and practices that have since lost their lustre because they are too detached from the very essence that gave the first communities their dynamism and life to the full. Returning to the sources does not mean turning back. It is to draw upon the spiritual legacy of a religious tradition, the living core that made it come to life and accomplished the miracle of improving the lives of women and men throughout the ages.

In 2007 we celebrated the thirtieth anniversary of the coming of John Main to Montreal as well as the twenty-fifth anniversary of his early death. Let us give thanks for all he has accomplished. Let us celebrate by closely examining the teaching of Christian meditation that has generated, and that still generates, such love for God in those who practise it. Let us thank God who speaks in 'the still small voice' and reveals himself in the attentive silence of our hearts.

Notes

1 Paul Harris (ed.), *Christian Meditation by Those Who Practice It*, Dimension Books, 1993.

2 Paul Harris, *John Main by Those Who Knew Him*, Darton, Longman & Todd, 1991.

6

JOURNEY TO PERSONAL AND SOCIAL TRANSFORMATION

Balfour M. Mount

I would like to consider 'Personal and social transformation'. What does that phrase imply? Transformation *from* what? Transformation *to* what? In considering these questions, I will be doing so from the perspective of one who has been caring for the dying for 40 years as a surgical oncologist and palliative care physician, and also from the perspective of a cancer patient and family member of loved ones dying from cancer. These latter perspectives are undoubtedly shared by many.

I have been blessed by many cherished teachers along the way. One of my teachers, Phil Simmons, a young man dying from Lou Gehrig's disease, described the task we all face as 'the harrowing business of rescuing joy from heartbreak'. Phil may have summed up the essence of these reflections when he said:

> As I see it, we know we're truly grown up when we stop trying to fix people … Before we go fixing others, we must first accept and find compassion for ourselves. Doing so we may begin to find that others don't need 'fixing' so much as simple kindness. When we stop seeing the world as *a 'Problem' to be solved*, when *instead* we open our hearts to the mystery of our common suffering, we may find ourselves where we least expected to be: in a world transformed by love.[1]

So let us explore the borders that define our human frailty and fears and the messages of hope that we may find there. And let us start with a question: 'What determines good quality of life (QOL) and our experience of being healthy and whole?'

Research has shown that our generally held assumption that QOL depends on physical well-being is wrong! For example, in one study, two-thirds of cancer patients who were aware of their diagnosis (most were undergoing active treatment at the time) assessed their own health as 'very healthy' – including 12 who died during the study. Similarly, in a study of emotional well-being, people with malignant melanoma had levels of emotional well-being equal to the general population, while in a study of life satisfaction, seriously disabled people, including some paralysed following trauma, had life satisfaction levels equal to those of the general population. Thus QOL does not correlate with physical well-being.

If physical well-being doesn't determine our QOL, what does? Let us look at QOL more closely. QOL may be defined as subjective well-being. It is the answer to the questions, 'How is it going?', 'How are you doing?', 'How are you in yourself today?'

The quest for improved QOL colours our lives. Whether in sickness or in health, each of us experiences a daily shifting back and forth between the QOL extremes: anguish and suffering at one end, and a sense of integrity and wholeness at the other. In the 1960s, Cicely Saunders, the founder of the modern hospice movement, coined the term 'Total Pain', suggesting that how we experience suffering, even the most physical suffering (such as hitting your thumb with a hammer) is modified by all domains of human experience – physical, psychological, social, spiritual, existential and financial.

Some factors may decrease our suffering. They support a response shift towards integrity and wholeness, on the suffering/wellness continuum. Other factors may produce an increase in our sense of suffering, anguish and Total Pain. We might call the former QOL shift 'healing' and the latter 'wounding'. Let me introduce you to two of my teachers who prompted me to study the nature of healing and wounding in greater detail.

Chip, a bright, dynamic, gifted young man aged 30 was referred to me for radical surgery for his widespread testicular cancer. He was an elite athlete on our national ski team, and physically fit to a degree I could never achieve with several lifetimes of exercise! Following surgery and chemotherapy we hoped that he was cured. It was a definite possibility. Over the months that followed, however, his disease recurred and his physical magnificence melted in the face of his spreading cancer. Chip died one year after the surgery. During our last conversation, just before his death, he confided to me, 'You know Bal, this last year has been the best year of my life.' Astonishing. The *best* year? Of *that* life? He elaborated, 'You know, I've had a great life, but I've always been outwardly directed. This year, I've been stopped in my tracks; I've had time to look inward, and that has been the most exciting journey I have had!' On the day Chip said that, his QOL, as measured by the state-of-the-art QOL instrument at that time, was very low (4/10), whereas, by the same instrument he had had the highest possible QOL (10/10) every day of his life prior to illness! Clearly that QOL assessment tool was missing something important.

In contrast, a second patient, Mrs C, was referred to our Palliative Care Service because of pain due to breast cancer that had spread to her bones. It should have been easy to bring under control, but it wasn't. One day I sat down at her bedside and asked, 'Mrs C, when were you last well?' With great feeling she retorted, 'Do you mean physically?' 'No,' I answered, 'I mean in yourself.' 'Doctor,' she exploded, 'I have never been well a day in my life!' 'Well,' I asked, 'if we are body, mind and spirit, where do you think the problem has been?' Without hesitation she exclaimed, 'I have been sick in mind and spirit every day of my life!' She went on to tell me her story – about the blind alleys in her life; her childhood in Eastern Europe; the broken relationships; the failed dreams; the present strained relationship with her daughter, her only living family member. We never did get her pain under control. But I would suggest that failure was grounded more in her well-established life script than in the cancer that, in fact, ended her pain.

Here were two persons who were dying. One aged 30 who had physically dissolved to the point that he looked like he had come from a concentration camp – but who had no suffering; the other in her seventies with terrible suffering augmented by a lifelong pattern of despair.

It was evident to us that the inner life, the existential or spiritual domain played an important role in determining QOL. As a result, our team, under the leadership of Robin Cohen, designed the McGill QOL instrument (MQOL), the first QOL scale to assess the significance of these factors. What did we find? The significance of the existential or spiritual domain proved to be very great for people with serious illness. For example, in one study involving cancer patients, the existential or spiritual domain was found to be an important determinant of QOL throughout the illness, from diagnosis to palliative care; as important as any other factor measured. In a second study involving persons with HIV disease, the spiritual/existential domain did not play a significant role early in the illness, but when the person had AIDS it was the most significant contributor to QOL. It became clear that the existential/spiritual domain is a major determinant of QOL in severe illness. Let us now examine the nature of suffering in greater detail.

Suffering is subjective and personal; experienced by whole persons, not bodies; it may arise in any domain of the individual; it occurs with a perceived threat of destruction, or alienation of our ego from our deepest self – of head from heart; finally, suffering ends when the threat of destruction passes, or (as with Chip) a sense of integrity is otherwise restored. Thus suffering presents us with a paradox. I may have significant pain but no anguish, no suffering. Conversely, I may be symptom free and suffer terribly.

What core existential issues challenge us and thus may increase our suffering? In his book *Existential Psychotherapy*,[2] Irvin Yalom suggests that there are four: *death* (in the sense of existential obliteration); *isolation* (referring to the unbridgeable gap between self and others) – while we may all be as one, at a quantum level, only I can experience my birth and my death, only you yours; *freedom* (referring to the unnerving absence of external structure that is seen in 'the Sunday afternoon syndrome' and 'the retirement syndrome' – 'I'd know what I'm supposed to be doing right now if I was at work!'); and *meaning* (that is, the dilemma of meaning-seeking creatures such as we are, as we confront a cosmos that is potentially without meaning). Let us look more closely at meaning.

On being freed from Auschwitz, Viktor Frankl wrote *Man's Search for Meaning* in eight days, based on his experiences in the Nazi concentration camps. In it, he suggests that our search is not for fame, fortune or sex, but for meaning. He suggests that it is meaning that gives quality to life and notes five sources of meaning: things created or accomplished; things left as a legacy; things believed; things loved (people, places, music, books, ideas, and so on); and finally, suffering itself may be a source of meaning.

As we ponder the existential issues that frame our lives, life may seem overwhelming. We ask, 'Can I, with all I have to face, transcend suffering and find healing?' In response, Frankl challenges us in offering a remarkable assessment of our human potential, a statement of hope that we must conclude was hard-won, given the unimaginable hell out of which these words were forged. Frankl observed: 'Everything can be taken from a man but one thing: the last of human freedoms – to choose one's attitude in any given set of circumstances, to choose one's own way.' As I start to feel sorry for myself, feel trapped or a victim, I am forced to recognize that if Frankl could find such freedom in Auschwitz, surely I can find freedom in responding to my circumstances.

But many do not find healing. What separates them from those who do? My colleague Pat Boston and I carried out a qualitative research study with people experiencing life-threatening illness, to see if there are common themes that separate those who find healing and those who find wounding. Themes common across cases at the wounded end of the spectrum included:

1 A sense of isolation and being disconnected.
2 A crisis of meaning, an existential vacuum with an inability to find solace or peace in anything.
3 Anxious preoccupation with the future or ongoing ruminations about the past.
4 A sense of victimization.
5 A need to be in control.

Conversely, those towards the healing end of the QOL continuum, as they faced a life-threatening illness, were characterized by:

1 A sense of connection. This was experienced at four different levels by the study participants. For some there was an experience of:
    (a) a sense of increased connection to oneself – that is, the individuation of Carl Jung;
    (b) for some, a deep connection to others – the I-thou relating of Martin Buber;
    (c) still others experienced an increased sense of connection to the phenomenal world that we perceive through our five senses – as in music or the beauties of nature;
    (d) and for some there was an experience of increased connection to ultimate meaning (God, the Cosmos, quantum oneness, the More).
2 A sense of meaning in the context of illness and suffering.
3 A capacity to enter the present moment and find peace there.
4 An experience of sympathetic connection to their suffering.

5 Openness to potential in the moment that was greater than their need for control, enabling Frankl's choice, that is, the ability to choose their response to their dire situation.

Healing connections are foundational to our experience of QOL. Eric Cassell put it succinctly: 'Our intactness as persons, our coherence and integrity, come not only from intactness of the body but from the wholeness of the web of relationships with self and others.'[3] Healing connections enable transcendence – an experience of entry into community with something greater and more enduring than the self.

Whoever we are, the need to feel connected lies at the core of our being. Ken has been one of my most cherished teachers in this regard. A bank robber, referred to us from a maximum security prison, he had spent most of his 34 years behind bars. He certainly knew how to 'get in your face', as they say in prison. Defences well in place – his, mine – Ken was now dying with advanced cancer, yet he still radiated an aura of danger. But somehow our fears were set aside – mine, his – and we let each other in. Just a little at first, then friends, then soulmates. What did I learn from Ken? Among many lessons, 'Of him to whom much is given much shall be required.' How different the hands that Ken and I had been dealt in life. Ken was brilliant, but the deck had been stacked against him from the beginning. His mother was in prison when he was born; his father was an alcoholic. I, on the other hand, had had all life's benefits showered on me. And now, years later, I am often praised; Ken condemned. But through our healing connection I began to recognize more fully my own limitations and his vulnerability, grace and value. And as things evolved, to meet Ken became for me, paradoxically, to meet Christ.

If we are healers, we are at best wounded healers. Our effectiveness as a healer for another person comes not from our knowledge, power, wisdom and strength, but from the recognition of our own vulnerability. How we relate to ourselves and others determines our impact as healers. Each of us has an inner need and potential for healing.

The wounded healer potential within both sufferer and caregiver is activated by the experience of suffering and a profound awareness of personal vulnerability. This has been known for millennia. In ancient Greece, the symbol of the wounded healer was the centaur Chiron who through his own incurable wound became the greatest of healers. To be a healer, for myself or for others, I must seek to know my own woundedness. Eight hundred years ago Rumi wrote:

> Your defects are the way that glory gets manifested. Whoever sees clearly what's diseased in himself begins to gallop on the way ... Self complacency blocks the workmanship ... Don't turn your head. Keep looking at the bandaged place. That's where the light enters you.[4]

Eight hundred years later Leonard Cohen wrote:

> Ring the bells that still can ring.
> Forget your perfect offering.
> There is a crack in everything.
> That's how the light gets in.[5]

(Either Rumi has been reading Leonard Cohen, or Leonard Cohen, Rumi!) Similarly, Yo Yo Ma commented:

> We all have walls and limits and barriers. I think the message is to find your personal wall – the wall you come up against that you need to explore, because ultimately *that* becomes the speaking part of your medium. You dare go there and you come back to report on what that is. *Then* you have something to say.[6]

Like Rumi and Leonard Cohen, Yo Yo Ma suggests that our defects and limits may embody our unique potential. It depends, it would seem, on how we handle the dragons within. What are our options?

We are all familiar with the medieval iconography of St George. The *real* man slays his dragon! But, are we as familiar with St Margaret? Icons of St Margaret from the same period show us another potential. Having identified her dragon, St Margaret placed it on a leash. The great harpsichordist and conductor of baroque music, Trevor Pinnock, understood the implications of St Margaret's insights. He said:

> A lot of fears and doubts and demons assailed me, as they (still) do, and they all had to be dealt with, and *have* to be dealt with. And what I have realized now is that all those fears and doubts and demons have to be, and are inevitably, a part of my music and they're an essential part of the music because of my humanity. And it's only with the joining of the humanity and the music that it makes any sense at all.

But how does Maestro Pinnock put the dragon on a leash? He went on to say:

> The hardest lesson, the one I'm still trying to learn, is to accept all the imperfections; to not necessarily welcome the demons, but at least acknowledge them, and perhaps ask them if they wouldn't mind standing at the side of the stage while I'm giving a concert, rather that sitting inside the harpsichord, or on me.[7]

E. Paul Hovey has suggested that four characteristics of our inner dragons, defects, cracks, walls, limits, barriers, sins or blocks in the ego-Self axis, are: self-sufficiency instead of faith; self-will instead of submission; self-seeking instead of benevolence; self-righteousness instead of humility.

We can, it would seem, be a healing presence, for ourselves and for others. A healing presence impacts on both our sense of meaning and experience of connectedness. It doesn't necessarily involve religious belief, intentional action or return to physical health. Healing can involve both the adaptation to change, over time, and the potential to transcend suffering in the now, in the present moment. Healing occurs both as an adaptive narrative process over time and in the eternal present of this moment, and this one, and this one. The option is always available to us! A person can die healed.

Healing involves:

- *volition*, an active initiation of the process on our part, a leap of faith, a stepping out in trust. There is an internal locus of control. No one can do it for us.
- *presence*, being attentive and aware, a coming into the present moment, into the now. The problem is that we are usually pre-occupied by the past or the future. We are rarely fully present to the moment at hand! Complete presence characterizes certain moments of awe, for example when we become fully aware of the beauty or grandeur of nature – perhaps the vastness of the sea or mountains, or sunlight on a field of grain. Lovers are healing to each other, in part, because they are fully present to each other.
- *opening* – to suffering, to descent into the unknown, to others.
- *accepting*, where that is understood as an active integration of reality, not as passive giving up ('Ah, so that's the way my cookie crumbled. Now, what am I going to do with it?').
- *humility*, the humility that is born in recognition of, and ac-ceptance of, my own limitations and shortcomings; a humility that recognizes that we are all in the same boat – *exactly the same boat;* a humility that removes any illusion of a power dif-ferential between us.
- *letting go* or, as Phil Simmons expressed it, 'learning to fall'. As we learn to fall, we let go of our attachment to illusions of con-

trol; we fall from head to heart, from ego to deep centre, from a stance of fearful quest for control and protective closure to one of opening to mystery and an experience of the unity of all things.

We need to come to recognize the healing potential within us, a potential that was, and is, and always shall be, the essence of our being. As C. S. Lewis observed:

> The process of living seems to consist in coming to realize truths so ancient and simple that, if stated, they sound like barren platitudes. They cannot sound otherwise to those who have not had the relevant experience: that is why there is no real teaching of such truths possible and every generation starts from scratch.[8]

In our quest for healing the real teacher is experience. But how do we know this isn't all just theory? We know because of the teachers we are blessed to meet along the way who show us where the process of healing might lead. We see the features of wholeness in those occasional persons who grace this world, giving us a sense of what wholeness might be like. I will mention two:

- Yo Yo Ma, to whom I have already referred. To observe him in concerts, or while he is exploring any of his many interests, is to note that he initiates contact by acknowledging the person with the least power in that setting. The pedestal that others place him on thus dissolves and true dialogue between equals is possible. He is so present to all others around him, so joyful, so light and alert. When asked if he realized that he is a great healer, he responded, 'Healing? I think that is what the music is all about. Don't you?'

- H. H. the Dalai Lama. In His Holiness we find a humility born not out of a belief system, but out of his moment-to-moment experience of his own connectedness to all other sentient

97

beings: his balance in body, mind and spirit; his insatiable interest in science and the world around him; his joy; his simple response to being asked about his religion. ('My religion is the practice of compassion.')

And as A. A. Milne might have said, 'It's the Tiddley Pom Principle!' ('The more it snows Tiddley Pom, the more it goes Tiddley Pom, the more it goes Tiddley Pom, on snowing!'[9]) For healing begets healing, begets healing and wounding begets wounding, begets wounding. Whether the agent is Hitler, Nelson Mandela or you and I, we are catalysts in an ongoing process that is beyond our anticipation. How important for us to keep that it mind.

Where will our personal quest for healing lead us? Where does my path lie? Where does yours? My path was introduced to me by another of my patients, another teacher – the Benedictine monk John Main. We cared for John on our Home Care Service while he was dying with cancer. He opened for me a window on the practice of meditation. As he stated more than once, 'I don't claim meditation is the *only* path toward healing, it's just the only path I know.'[10]

John Main observed:

We are not people who have to live on the surface, or people who are condemned to live lives of shallow emotions. Meditating is leaving the shallows, leaving the surface, and entering into the depths of your own being. Its purpose is to advance along the way of the fullness of your own humanity.[11]

In like manner, quantum mechanics physicist David Bohm concluded: 'What is needed is to learn afresh, to observe, and to discover for ourselves, the meaning of wholeness.'[12] Walt Whitman exclaimed in wonderment, 'I am large; I contain multitudes.'[13]

In discovering our potential for integrity and wholeness, we are glimpsing what healing might be like. In *The Velveteen Rabbit*,

Margery Williams reminds us that the process of healing is the process of becoming Real.

> The Skin Horse had lived longer in the nursery than any of the others. He was so old that his brown coat was bald in patches and showed the seams underneath, and most of the hairs in his tail had been pulled out to string bead necklaces …
>
> ---
>
> 'What is REAL?' asked the Rabbit one day, when they were lying side by side near the nursery fender, before Nana came to tidy the room. 'Does it mean having things that buzz inside you and a stick-out handle?' 'Real isn't how you are made,' said the Skin Horse. 'It's a thing that happens to you. When a child loves you for a long, long time, not just to play with, but REALLY loves you, then you become Real.' 'Does it hurt?' asked the Rabbit. 'Sometimes,' said the Skin Horse, for he was always truthful. 'When you are Real you don't mind being hurt.' 'Does it happen all at once, like being wound up,' he asked, 'or bit by bit?'
>
> 'It doesn't happen all at once,' said the Skin Horse. 'You become. It takes a long time. That's why it doesn't often happen to people who break easily, or have sharp edges, or who have to be carefully kept. Generally, by the time you are Real, most of your hair has been loved off, and your eyes drop out and you get loose in the joints and very shabby. But these things don't matter at all, because once you are Real you can't be ugly, except to people who don't understand.'[14]

In closing, let us recall Frankl's choice: 'Everything can be taken from a man but one thing: the last of human freedoms – to choose one's attitude in any given circumstances, to choose one's own way.'[15] How sobering, how glorious, to discover that we can claim Viktor Frankl's 'last of human freedoms' as our own. The choice is ours!

Notes

1 Comments on healing from Philip Simmons's wonderful book, *Learning to Fall: The Blessings of an Imperfect Life*, Bantam Books, 2002.

2 Irvin Yalom, *Existential Psychotherapy*, New York, Basic Books, 1980.

3 E. J. Cassell, *The Nature of Suffering and the Goals of Medicine*, New York, Oxford University Press, 1991, p. 40.

4 Rumi, *The Essential Rumi*, trans. Coleman Barks with John Moyne, New York, HarperCollins, 1995, pp. 141–2.

5 L. Cohen, 'Anthem', in Stranger Music: Selected Poems and Songs, Stranger Music, Inc., 1992; and on *Leonard Cohen The Future*, Columbia CK 53226. Used by permission.

6 Yo Yo Ma, *In Performance*, CBC interview with Eric Friesen, 26 September 1999.

7 T. Pinnock, keynote address, 15th International Congress on Care of the Terminally Ill, Montreal, 22 September 2004.

8 C. S. Lewis, from a letter to Dom Bede Griffiths, 8 May 1939.

9 A. A. Milne, 'The Tiddely-Pom Principle', cited by Benjamin Hoff, in *The Tao of Pooh*, New York, Penguin Books, 1982, p. 134.

10 John Main, personal communication, Benedictine Priory of Montreal, 1988.

11 John Main, 'The Purpose of Meditation', in *Coming Home: An Introductory Seminar to Christian Meditation*, London, The World Community for Christian Meditation, Section 1: What is Meditation in the Christian Tradition.

12 D. Bohm, *Wholeness and the Implicate Order*, London, Routledge & Kegan Paul, 1980.

13 W. Whitman, *Leaves of Grass*, 1892.

14 M. Williams, *The Velveteen Rabbit*, New York, Avon Books, 1975, pp. 16–17.

15 V. Frankl, *Man's Search for Meaning*, New York, Simon & Shuster, 1959, p. 86.

7

FROM JOHN CASSIAN TO JOHN MAIN

Reflections on Christian Meditation

Adalbert de Vogüé

The writings of John Cassian played a decisive role in the life of John Main. It was thanks to a page of the *Conferences* that, at the age of 45, he was finally able to fuse the two elements which made up his personal spirituality and which had until then been unintegrated.

He related the story some years later in *The Gethsemani Talks*.[1] He was initiated in his youth to Hindu 'meditation' and was formed by the repetition of a unifying mantra. On becoming a Benedictine monk (in 1959) he had renounced this practice which was so simple and beneficial, and adopted under obedience the method of Western prayer (the production of various 'acts') which was taught at the novitiate at Ealing. For 12 years or more he had thus been separated from the spiritual source which had nourished him in the beginning and had fallen little by little into a certain spiritual void, filled, and at the same time emptied, by activism.

However, in the midst of his demanding activities at Washington (1969–74), a providential meeting compelled him to reread Baker's *Holy Wisdom* and this led him to Cassian. In Conference X, with amazement, he discovered the principle of repeating a phrase in order to reach continual prayer. His rediscovery of the basic practice learned from his Indian master, in an author expressly recommended by St Benedict, allowed him to re-form the unity of his spiritual being on this practice, by reconciling these two elements: the wisdom acquired in India and the gift of self in Christian monasticism, the experience of Eastern meditation and loyalty to the Benedictine tradition.

The role of mediator played by Cassian in Main's story is interesting in several ways. First of all, in the historical dimension it offers an example of having recourse to a pre-Benedictine author to enrich and correct the post-Benedictine tradition. As Baker had already done – but somewhat differently, as we shall see – Main returns to a source of the Rule to supply for a lacuna in it which is left open or imperfectly filled by those who make use of it.

In another dimension, that of space, this story unexpectedly continues the great mission of mediator which fell to Cassian. From their first appearance, the invaluable service rendered by the *Institutes* and *Conferences* had been to transmit to the West a wisdom which was Egyptian, Oriental and Greek. In the case of Main this meeting between East and West expands beyond the Christian East to include the pagan Far East. Thanks to Cassian – who would have believed it? – a Hindu practice finds the right to be applied in Christianity.

This means that Cassian, on this as on other occasions, established himself as a remarkable ecumenist. By proposing to Latin monks, in the name of Egyptian monasticism, a formula of prayer to be repeated without ceasing, the author of Conference X does not only build a bridge between two regions of the Christian world of his time. Without knowing it, he puts his Western readers in communication with two other traditions that will span the centuries: Hinduism with its mantra – as we have just said – and Greek *hesychasm* with its 'Jesus prayer'. And so there appears, on a vast geographical and temporal scale, a real unity of monastic spiritual experience. Apparently independent of each other the Egyptian monasticism of the fourth century, later Byzantine monasticism and Hindu spirituality of all times discovered and employed this kind of mystical law. As spokesman for the monks of Egypt to their brothers in the West, Cassian has not been merely a witness of this unity: he can be also – as Main proves to us – its effective servant.

Cassian's role as liaison in this matter is all the more essential as Latin monasticism has not produced a phrase analogous to the Jesus Prayer, nor has it even used any other Christian mantra in a sustained way. It is something strange and cause for regret that the *Deus in adiutorium* recommended by Abbot Isaac has as far as we know not been used in the West in the way the author of the *Conferences* suggested. No echo has come to us of a school of spirituality which cultivated it as a phrase for continual prayer. Instead of this unceasing, personal practice at which Cassian aimed, we find only examples of liturgical or ritual use, whether in the Rule of St Benedict himself,[2] or in his contemporary and countryman Cassiodorus,[3] or in the Franco-Celtic monasticism of the following century.[4] 'These do witness indeed to the fact that the message of Abbot Isaac was heard: the verse he recommended is greatly respected and its richness of meaning is perceived. But it is not used for continuous prayer. The very end which Cassian had in mind has been lost sight of.

In the absence of Cassian's *Deus in adiutorium* which was diverted to other purposes, did Latin Christianity of the Middle Ages use other equivalent formula-phrases for repetition? Perhaps they waited some centuries, until the invention of the rosary, to use a similar method in a regular way. In the Master and in Benedict we do find invitations to say one or another word 'without ceasing in his heart'.[5] But the very fact that they recommend the repetition of several different phrases shows that they did not mean a real practice of continual repetition which presupposes the choice of a single text. The end of these phrases to 'say without ceasing' was not to support continual prayer but to inculcate certain attitudes of vigilance or of humility which the Master and Benedict held to be particularly necessary.

Latin monasticism has thus been deprived of any formula of prayer and that is why Conference X stands as a witness of such high importance. In fact only this teaching of Abbot Isaac reminds the monks of the West of a method of perpetual prayer which they have not been able to put into practice. It is a bitter paradox that the most ancient testimony of such a practice is in Latin and that it has been completely neglected by the Latin world. But Main's example shows that the foundation laid by Cassian was not in vain. Thanks to the author of the *Conferences* the *monologistos* prayer, as it was to be called by the monks of the East, belongs for ever to the treasury of the Western tradition, and nothing prevents the sons of Benedict from drawing it from there for their own profit, among the other *nova et vetera*.[6]

Although the connection between Cassian and Main is of interest for various reasons, it merits also to be considered for itself. How did Main understand Cassian? What precisely did he retain of Conference X? Is his interpretation rigorously exact or relatively free?

When we consider closely the many references to Cassian in *The Gethsemani Talks*, we become aware, first, of a few accidents. One of these misinterpretations is without doubt due to the translation Main was using[7] and it is moreover of no significance. But another does seem attributable to Main himself. According to him, the term 'catholic', which occurs several times in the first chapters of the Conference,[8] refers to the method of prayer extolled in the last chapters, that is, the 'prayer of poverty', which consists in the repeating of a single verse.[9] Actually, when Isaac speaks of 'the catholic faith', of 'the interpretation of the catholic churches', or of 'the faith of the catholic tradition', he had in mind only the interpretation of the great text of Genesis which makes of man 'the image of God'. This orthodox exegesis of Genesis 1.26, which is opposed to the anthropomorphism of the old Serapion, has no direct bearing on the formula of prayer revealed at the end of the Conference.

This confusion is no doubt due to the quick way in which Main treats his subject in these simple talks. One can explain similarly other minor errors.[10] When allowance is made for these excusable approximations we see that Main has grasped an essential part of Isaac's teaching: the constant repetition of a phrase is a way to become 'poor in spirit' and thereby to discover the infinite riches of the kingdom of God.[11]

On the other hand, what Main did not retain is the special value of the particular phrase that Abbot Isaac proposed. In fact, for Cassian the great secret of the Egyptian monk does not consist in the repetition of any formula but precisely of the one he proposes: *Deus in adiutorium meum intende, Domine ad adiuvandum me festina.* (Ps. 69.2). This verse literally possesses all virtues. If it is suited to nourish continual prayer, it is because, by its generality, it expresses the fundamental need which human beings in their fragility and sinfulness experience in every situation.[12] By repeating it we become 'poor', not only because the mind is reduced to a single thought but also because we recognize ourselves as powerless, needy of grace, 'God's beggars'. To put it another way, the 'poverty' that it brings us to concerns humility,[13] as much as simplified thought. If Main did not attach particular importance to the contents of Isaac's phrase but only retained the principle of repeating a phrase, this can be easily explained by considering the Hindu tradition of the mantra, which is somewhat undetermined and left to the choice of the meditator. Moreover, this tradition recommends brief phrases 'of one to fifteen syllables, nearly always less than twelve'.[14] With 25 syllables the *Deus in adiutorium* of Cassian exceeds these limits.[15] Without criticizing it, Main has quietly put it aside. A detail of translation illustrates this silent rejection: when Cassian speaks of 'this verse', Main translates 'a single verse'.[16]

An accurate appreciation of the relationship of Main to Cassian demands that we take a broader look at Cassian's ideas and intentions in the last chapters of Conference X. This is the last of the ten talks from Scete and with the preceding it forms the conclusion of the first series of *Conferences*, recalling by certain of its features the first two talks, those of Abbot Moses.[17] In the same way that Conference IX newly presents, under the name of 'prayer', the ideal of contemplation proposed in Conference I, so Conference X, by dealing with the infallible means to arrive at this end, walks in the steps of Conference II. According to Moses, the sure way to go straight towards the end, outwitting every ruse of the devil, is discretion. According to Isaac, the sure way to pray without ceasing – and also, as we shall see, to overcome every impure spirit – is to repeat in every situation the verse *Deus in adiutorium*.

Just as for Moses discretion consisted in guarding against opposite forms of excess – both too much and too little – so the *Deus in adiutorium* is extolled by Isaac as the supreme weapon against opposite temptations – to eat or sleep too much or not to eat or sleep at all –[18] and then in the same vein as the appropriate prayer in opposite situations, whether disturbing or favorable: temptations of lust or the absence of temptations, feelings of pride or a sense of humility, dryness or spiritual joy, terrors of the night or security,[19] in a word, as the phrase to be repeated in the same way 'when things are going badly, to be delivered, and also when things are going well, to be kept in that state and preserved from pride'.[20]

In the midst of these coupled antitheses, Isaac slips in a listing of three vices: anger, avarice and sadness.[21] Together with the preceding ones (gluttony and lust) and the following ones (acedia, vanity and pride), these three occasions in which to recite the *Deus in adiutorium* form an almost perfectly arranged complete list of the eight principal vices, as they were described in the last eight books of the *Institutes* and in Conference V. This is a significant point: Cassian here sums up the battle against the vices, which for him constitutes 'practical (or active) knowledge' – what today we call asceticism – and the indispensable foundation of all contemplation.[22]

In this conclusion to the first *Conferences*, the *Deus in adiutorium* thus plays a triple role: as a universal remedy against the vices, it is, like discretion, the weapon par excellence of the active life; as a prayer appropriate for every situation, it is the perfect instrument for continuous prayer, and so for the contemplative life; as a cry for help, it means humility and acknowledgement of divine grace, poverty which leads to the knowledge of God.[23] The verse has this triple function because of its particular content. It is not by chance that Isaac – or Cassian – selected it from all the verses of the Psalter, indeed of the entire Scriptures, to make of it a *formula orationis* comparable to the Lord's Prayer itself.[24]

These various aspects that made the *Deus in adiutorium* a synthesis of the first *Conferences* are absent in Main's reading of the Cassian-Isaac text. He retains only one recommendation: the 'impoverishment' of thoughts concentrated by the continuous repetition of the word.[25]

No doubt Cassian attached a great importance to the unifying power of the phrase but that power was not restricted to it. The whole treatise on prayer, which makes up the *Conferences* of Abbot Isaac, is given rhythm by an ebb and flow movement from the multiple to the single. After the four kinds of prayer listed by the Apostle,[26] there first comes a unifying by the prayer of fire.[27] By then ascending to the Lord's Prayer we again find the multiplicity of its seven petitions,[28] but this is again mastered by the unspeakable simplicity of the prayer of fire, then described for the second time.[29]

These two progressions towards the one, which gives its structure to Conference IX, have a third added to them, which is itself divided into two parts in Conference X. This time we pass, first, from 'the richness and profusion of all thoughts' to the poverty of *Deus in adiutorium* repeated without ceasing. From there we are raised to 'the multiform knowledge of God',[30] that is, to an experiential knowledge of all that the Scriptures, and especially the Psalter, describe.[31] Finally, this richness is itself reduced to unity in the prayer of fire, which Cassian described for a third time, while referring to his preceding descriptions.[32]

The passage from 'the richness of thoughts' to the 'poverty' of a single work, alone retained by Main, is only one of the four returns to unity which mark the *De Oratione* of Cassian.[33] If the English Benedictine is concerned with this point exclusively, it is because it relates to his or her own experience of the benefits of *japa*,[34] that is, of the repetition of the mantra. The only thing he is asking from Cassian – and that with good reason – is the Christian authentication of this Hindu practice.

Moreover, he is in no way trying to smuggle in under the umbrella of the *Conferences*, a commodity foreign to Christianity. As much as we may be disturbed by the way in which too many Christians use the spiritual techniques of the Far East,[35] that of Main gives an impression of absolute Christian authenticity. It is not his least merit – one due, no doubt, to his solid monastic formation – that he had perfectly assimilated Hindu meditation into a religious life that was entirely given over to Christ.

Mention has just been made of Main's Benedictine formation. It should be pointed out that it offered him a base for his later rediscovery of the mantra, which was no less important than the *Deus in adiutorium* of Cassian. I refer to the daily half-hour of prayer which his Congregation gave him as an obligation.[36] This time set apart for meditation corresponds precisely to what Main practised with his Hindu master. In Cassian there is no mention of this half-hour of mental prayer, which is a modern idea based on certain suggestions of the Rule. One can say that Main's Christian *japa* consists in filling the half-hour meditation of contemporary Benedictinism with the repetition of a phrase in the way practised by the early monks.

According to Abbot Isaac there was no special time set aside for the practice of this repetition. One should say the *Deus in adiutorium* at all times,[37] without pre-determined frequency, or stopping other activities. One's whole existence was thus to be permeated by the continuously repeated phrase, and this was prescribed with reference to the famous *Shema* of Judaism or, rather, of the Bible itself: 'You will repeat it sitting at home and travelling on the road, sleeping and waking; you will write it on your threshold and the doors of your mouth; you will put it on the walls of your house and in the depths of your heart …'[38] In thus paraphrasing Deuteronomy, Isaac showed the free and undetermined character of the repetition that he advocated and at the same time found a useful scriptural precedent for it.

The two half-hour periods of meditation, morning and evening, of which Main speaks, obviously do not exclude this day-long occasional and spontaneous repetition. On the contrary, they call for it as a natural and indeed indispensable complement. Even though he does not speak of it directly Main lets it be understood in passing.[39] A life of prayer needs both special times when one does only that, and a continual mindfulness preserved throughout all one's occupations.[40]

For his rediscovery of the mantra Main is therefore indebted to modern Benedictinism as well as to Cassian. Moreover, was it not Dom Augustine Baker, the great spiritual writer of the English Benedictine Congregation, who prompted his rereading of the *Conferences* and rediscovery of the secret of Abbot Isaac? To complete this summary of the relationship of Main with Cassian, it would be useful to consider the relationship of Baker with the author of the *Institutes* and the *Conferences*. Baker does not seem ever to quote the prayer-phrase of Abbot Isaac in *Sancta Sophia*. Once however – and Main does not miss it[41] – he seems to allude to it in speaking of 'the ejaculatory prayers mentioned and rightly recommended by the holy hermits in Cassian'.[42] According to him, these 'are in reality "infused aspirations", the effects which flow from the already acquired habit of continuous prayer, and not imperfect preparations for it'.

Whatever there may have been in this reading in which Main recognized 'an intuitive understanding of the mantra', the repetition of a phrase is not what had caught Baker's attention in Cassian. Rather than precise suggestions of this kind he searched the *Conferences* for general inspiration to validate the interior life and mystical prayer. In fact, his major concern was to introduce into the Benedictine milieu of his time a mysticism that was mainly dependent on the works of medieval and modern spirituality, as his list of authors shows.[43] Cassian interested him above all for the relationship he was able to establish between the spiritual world of the Rule and more recent mystical expression. The author of the *Conferences* served Baker in much the same way he did Main, as authority and intermediary, though in a broader way and in regard to a different tradition.

As this is Baker's perspective, we can understand why he quotes the *Institutes*[44] far less than the *Conferences*, and that he principally garners from these the teachings of Abbot Isaac. Two of the three descriptions of the prayer of fire are quoted by him *in extenso*.[45] Twice also he quotes the solemn affirmation of Conferences IX and X – the end and perfection of the monk is in prayer.[46] Of this prayer that Isaac extols, he highlights both its continuousness and its sublimity and purity[47] that allow for no distractions.[48]

Around these quotations from the two talks on prayer Baker arranges some remarks found elsewhere and illustrating related themes. One of the *Conferences* provides a phrase to support 'the need for direct divine inspiration',[49] another an example of ecstatic prayer.[50] But it is Conference XXIII above all that Baker exploits because it presents contemplation as the sole occupation that is perfectly holy and free from sin,[51] thus placing the interior soul in the same relation to the imperfect one as a clear-sighted to a short-sighted person.[52]

Baker puts forward this high ideal of interior perfection and contemplative prayer to Benedictine monks with force, basing it on the referral to the *Conferences* which he found in the Rule.[53] He treats seriously the declarations Benedict makes about his own work and asserts that the Rule by its modest regulations aims to make souls capable of accepting these more advanced teachings. By itself, the Rule does not bring perfection, nor does it pretend to. Monks who see nothing beyond it are like the two young cenobites of Bethlehem, Cassian and Germanus, before their visit to the anchorites of Egypt when they were unaware of 'the true spirit of contemplative prayer … the pure spiritual prayer free of images'.[54]

This way of understanding the Benedictine Rule and cenobitical formation is analogous to Main's, which is why it was worthwhile to sketch Baker's approach to both Benedict and Cassian. Across four centuries, these two English Benedictines have followed similar routes. From the Rule of St Benedict as the fundamental law of their Congregation, they both moved, the first guiding the second, to that great work which Benedict himself made the pattern of reading for the Community meetings of his monks. And in the *Conferences* they both went to the heart of the work: the *De Oratione* of Abbot Isaac. There they found, each in his own manner, an invitation to follow a most demanding way of prayer.

In concluding this homage to John Cassian and John Main, allow me to say how I have profited from the lesson of each. In September 1977 when I was visiting the monasteries of Ireland, a monk of Glenstal noticed in certain of my presentations a similarity with *The Gethsemani Talks*, and he gave me a typewritten copy of them to read. The talks were going to appear some weeks later in *Cistercian Studies*.

In fact, when I was asked to speak on prayer or on *lectio* I used to expound on what seemed to me to be the sole method of prayer of the monks of old: first of all, to listen to God in his Word, read or recited by heart, then to respond to him in prayer. The *meditatio* of the ancient monks – the oral recitation of Scripture – was the continuation, throughout the hours of work and other activities, of this listening to the divine Word heard during the time of *lectio*. This made it possible to respond in prayer at all times, thus sustaining the continual prayer which is the 'goal of the monk'.

This practice of the early monks, which I recalled for my audience with particular reference to the witness of Cassian, is unfortunately difficult for our times, in face of the inadequate training of our memories and the nature of our often excessively absorbing works. For this reason I tried to adapt it to our contemporary capacity by proposing to reduce the recitation of the Scriptures to the repetition of a single word: for example, some words of a psalm, impressed on the memory in the morning during the traditional 'half-hour' and then recited throughout the day.

This system, which I had practised for several years and still do today, to some degree identifies with the Jesus Prayer of Eastern monasticism and the *Deus in adiutorium* of Cassian. To these two traditional references, which were the only ones I was then able to give, there could be added the Indian mantra Christianized by John Main. I was greatly struck by this convergence of independent monastic experiences, which points to the universal need for a centre of mental unity, where the mind may at any time recollect itself and resituate itself in the presence of God.

In my modest effort at 'meditation' I experimented with that unifying quality of a phrase repeated throughout the day. However, I did not go as far as repeating the same phrase each day. At the beginning of each day I changed the phrase taking the words which the Psalter offered me as they came. My system of meditation then was half-way between the recital of whole pages of Scripture, as practised by the Egyptian cenobites described by Cassian, and the unceasing repetition of the same word recommended by Abbot Isaac, the Byzantine Hesychasts and Hinduism. This added a certain variety to the benefit of an interior unity. This was surely not the absolute 'poverty' extolled by Cassian and so dear to Main. But was not the Scripture given to us in its rich variety so that we could be endlessly filled with these riches?

I would not propose this quite personal variant of the classical practice as an example to be followed. If I write of it here it is certainly not to compete with the great methods recommended by the masters and consecrated by tradition, but only to say what I owe to Cassian and to Main. The first has made me understand, better than any ancient author, the true place of Scripture, both read and recited, in the attempt at continual prayer. And by the example of his *Deus in adiutorium* he has prompted me to reduce the scriptural recitation to the repetition of a few words. The latter has strengthened me in this way above all by showing me that, as I do, others use the 'half-hours of prayer' morning and evening for the simple repetition of a word or a phrase.

Methods serve us, and each person ought to make his or her own, with the actual data of his or her own nature and background. But we can all profit from the lesson of our predecessors and contemporaries. For me, as for many others without doubt, John Cassian and John Main have been two of those salutary brethren and for this, after God, I would like to thank them.

Notes

[Since this article was written, many of the titles quoted in the *Notes* have been reissued. Visit www.MedioMedia.org online to order the latest editions.]

1 John Main, *Christian Meditation: The Gethsemani Talks*, Montreal, Benedictine Priory of Montreal, 1977 (we cite the 2nd edn, 1982). A first version, somewhat abridged, appeared in three parts in *Cistercian Studies* 12 (1977), 184–90, 272–81; 13 (1978), 75–83, under the significant title, 'Prayer in the Tradition of John Cassian', to which the second and third parts prefix the words 'Christian Meditation'.

2 *Regula Benedicti* (*RB*) 17, 3 and 18, 1 (office); 35, 17 (ritual).

3 Cassiodorus, *Comm. Psal.* 69, 2. See my publication *La Règle de Saint Benoît*. Tome VI, Paris, 1971 (Sources Chrétienne (*SC*) 186), p. 1029.

4 Columban, *Reg. Coen.* 9 (158, 13–21 Walker); Donat, Reg. 34, 7. Cf. de Vogué, *La Règle de Saint Benoît*, Tome V, Paris 1971 (*SC* 185), p. 583.

5 *Regula Magistri* (*RM*) 10, 19 = *RB* 7, 18 (Ps. 17.24); *RM* 10, 85 = *RB* 7, 65 (*Oratio Manasse* 9: cf. Matt. 8.8, Luke 18.13). To these formulas of the first and twelfth degrees of humility is added a seventh degree (*RM* 10, 71; cf. *RB* 7, 54), but this composite text (Ps. 118.71, 73) is not 'to say without ceasing' as in the Master, who furthermore omits 'in his heart'. With regard to Benedict, his very abridged introduction no longer speaks of repetition. The most interesting of these three formulations is that of the twelfth degree, put in the mouth of the Publican in the Gospel in place of 'Propitius esto mihi peccatori', which becomes, as we know, one of the two elements of the Jesus Prayer. Cf. my article 'La Règle de Saint Benoît et la Vie Contemplative', in *Saint Benoît: Sa Vie et sa Règle*, Vie Monastique 12 (Bellefontaine, 1981), 149–50.

6 Cf. my article 'Preghiera', in *Dizionario degli Instituti di Perfezione* 7 (1983), col. 603, translated under the title 'Prayer in Early Monasticism', *Word and Spirit* 3 (1983), 106–20 (see 115–16).

7 Cf. *Christian Meditation*, p. 19: 'I do not think I shall have any difficulty in introducing you into what I may call the hall (of prayer) for you to roam about its recesses as the Lord may direct,' translating Conference X, 9, 2: 'nec me laboraturum credo, ut iam intra aulam quodammodo ipsius oberrantes in adyta quoque, in quantum dominus direxerit, introducam'; the word 'iam', neglected by this translation, gives the sentence a different sense, correctly rendered by E. Pichery in Jean Cassian, *Conferences VIII – XVII*, Paris, 1958 (*SC* 54), 84. (We cite henceforth the Latin text of this edition, adding the paragraph division of Petschenig in *CSEL* 13). Main reproduces here, with few variants, the translation of E. C. S. Gibson in *The Nicene and Post-Nicene Fathers*, Vol. XI, Ser. 2, Grand Rapids, Eerdmans, 1982, 405.

8 Conference X, 1 (catholicae fidei); 3, 2 (catholicae … ecclesiae); 3, 3 (fidem catholicae traditionis). See also Conference X, 5, 3 (catholicis dogmatibus).

9 See Conference X, pp. 19–21.

10 *Christian Meditation*, p. 18, Main puts the departure of Cassian and Germanus in relation to the arrival of Jerome in Bethlehem, 'accompanied by a storm of intellectual controversies'; the hypothesis is more amusing than well founded. Page 21 n. 9; the reference is to Conference X, 10, 14–15. Page 38, 'pax perniciosa' is not found in Conference X, 8, 5, but in Conference IV, 7, 2, where it is not a question of prayer but the antagonism between flesh and spirit; with regard to the 'Sopor letalis' (Conference X, 8, 5), these words aim at, in Cassian, a state of distraction (worldly thoughts), rather than 'floating prayer' (in the absence of the prayer-phrase), which makes one think more readily of Conference X, 13, 1–2.

11 Conference X, 11, 1 (Matt. 5.3), cited on pp. 17 and 33 (see pp. 35 and 53).

12 Conference X, 10.

13 See Conference X, 11, 2. Further on (11, 3–4), Cassian gives evidence of other aspects of this humility: 'simplicity' and 'weakness' (non-resistance to evil).

14 J. Herbert, *Spiritualité Hindoue*, Paris, 1947, p. 366.

15 Cited 16 times in Conference X, 10, the verse is always reproduced in extenso. Apart from its excessive length, his usage is distinguished from that of mantras by a trait which we speak about again (n. 37 infra): one does not repeat it during a time reserved for meditation, but throughout the myriad activities of the day and night.

16 'Versiculi huius' (Conference X, 11, 1), translated by Gibson (p. 407) 'this one verse', and by Main (*Christian Meditation*, p. 33), 'a single verse'.

17 Cf. our article, 'Pour comprendre Cassien: un survol des Conférences', *Coll. Cist.* 39 (1977), 250–72 (see 259–60). A translation appeared in *Cistercian Studies* 19 (1984).

18 Conference X, 10, 6–8.

19 Conference X, 10, 9–13.

20 Conference X, 10, 14.

21 Conference X, 10, 10.

22 See Conference XIV, 1–2.

23 Conference X, 11, 2. Cf. Conference 111, 11–22, a comprehensive treatise on grace, foreshadowing Conference XIII and XXIII; Conference V, 15, etc.

24 Formula used in speaking of the Lord's Prayer (Conference IX, 18, 2 and 22, 1), as well as of 'Deus in adiutorium' (Conference X, 8, 5; 10, 1–2 and 14, 11, 1).

25 Conference X, 11, 1.

26 Conference IX, 9–15 commenting on 1 Tim. 2.1.

27 Conference IX, 15, 2. The conclusion (15, 3 and 16–17) treats once more the four types, joined together in John 17 and Phil. 4.6 (Conference IX, 17, 3–4).

28 Conference IX, 18–24.

29 Conference IX, 25.

30 Conference X, 11, 2 (mentioned by Main, *Christian Meditation*, p. 35).

31 Conference X, 11, 4–6 (cf. Main, p. 44). One is reminded of Evagrius, *De or.* 85, which makes the 'varied forms of wisdom' (cf. Eph. 3.10) the characteristic of psalmody, by contrast to the 'intangible and uniform

wisdom' which characterizes prayer. See also Athanasius, *Ep. ad Marcellum*: the Psalter is a mirror which reflects all the states of the soul.

32 Conference X, 11, 6.

33 To these ascending movements is added that of Conference X, 6: from the vision of Jesus, earthly man, in the 'active life' among men, to that of Christ glorified on the mountain in contemplative solitude. We note in this regard that John Main 'was, before his death, moving towards the fuller silence of the eremitical life' (*Christian Meditation*, p. 60).

34 On this term, see Herbert, *Spiritualité Hindoue*, pp. 366–9; Swami Siddheswarananda, *La Méditation selon le Yoga-Vedanta* (Paris, 1945), pp. 103, 146. Main, who does not use the term, seems to unite under the name of mantra, the phrase and its repetition.

35 See especially the collection *Des bords du Gange aux rives du Jourdain* (Paris, Fribourg, edn Saint Paul, 1983), with contributions by Hans Urs von Balthasar, Louis Bouyer, Olivier Clément, etc. One knows that the mantra recommended by Main is the Christian ejaculation 'Maranatha' (*Christian Meditation*, pp. 45–6). The meditation which he advocates leads, through Christ, to the Triune God who dwells within us.

36 See *Christian Meditation*, p. 14. Main does not indicate whether this half-hour was observed twice daily, morning and evening, as is the case in certain Benedictine congregations, and as he himself invites one to do.

37 Conference X, 10, 14 ('in all work, service, or travelling … in sleeping and eating, in satisfying the most humble natural needs') and 15 (going to sleep, walking, kneeling for prayer or rising, all types of work and action).

38 Conference X, 10, 15, paraphrasing Deut. 6.7–9.

39 See *Christian Meditation*, p. 50, in implicit reference to Conference X, 10, 15.

40 This principle, which was instilled by the venerable abbot who received me into the monastery 40 years ago, is well expressed by Swami Siddheswarananda, *La Méditation*, pp. 55, 103. Cf. Conference X, 14, 2: 'Perparum namque orat, quisquis illo tantum tempore, quo genua flectuntur orare consueuit.'

41 See *Christian Meditation*, p. 16.

42 Augustine Baker, *La Sainte Sapience*, Vol. 2, Paris, 1954 (Jr. 1, Part 1, ch. 4, sec. 10), p. 35. In looking over the pages of the French edition, the only one we have at hand, we indicate in parenthesis the reference to the passage (Treatise, Part, Chapter, Paragraph), which one will find the same in any English edition.

43 Baker, *La Sainte Sapience*, Vol. 1, p. 64 (Tr. I, Part 2, ch. 3, sec. 3).

44 Baker, *La Sainte Sapience*, Vol. 2, p. 161 (Tr. 3, Part 3, ch. 6, sec. 4),

citing Cassian, *Inst. Praef.* 8 (to adjust austerity to strength); Vol. 1, p. 253 Tr. 2, Part 2, ch. 6, sec. 1), which may allude to Institutes V, 13 (the first step in virtue is to master gluttony).

45   Baker, *La Sainte Sapience*, Vol. 2, p. 120 (Tr. 3, Part 3, ch. 2, sec. 4), citing Conference IX, 25; Vol. 2, p. 182 (Tr. 3, Part 4, ch. 1, sec. 5), citing Conference X, 11, 6.

46   Baker, *La Sainte Sapience*, Vol. 1, p. 133 (Tr. 1, Part 3, ch. 4, sec. 4), citing Conference IX, 7, 4 (this sentence of Germanus repeats approximately that of Isaac; see 2, 1) and X, 7, 3; Vol. 2, p. 32 (Tr. 3, Part 1, ch. 4, sec. 7), citing a new Conference X, 7, 3.

47   Baker, *La Sainte Sapience*, Vol. 1, p. 133 (Tr. 1, Part 3, ch. 4, sec. 4), citing Conference X, 5, 3 and IX, 31.

48   Baker, *La Sainte Sapience*, Vol. 2, p. 26 (Tr. 3, Part 1, ch. 3, sec. 5), citing Conference X, 14, 2.

49   Baker, *La Sainte Sapience*, Vol. 1, p. 74 (Tr. 1, Part 2, ch. 4, sec. 3), citing Conference III, 10, 6: magisterio (ipsius) et illuminatione (deducti) ad perfectionem (summae beatitudinis) peruenimus (cf. Conference III, 14). The following citation (quotidiana Domini illuminatione illustrata) remains to be identified.

50   Baker, *La Sainte Sapience*, Vol. 2, p. 32 (Tr. 3, Part I, ch. 4, sec. 7), citing Conference XIX, 4, 1 (John forgets to eat).

51   Baker, *La Sainte Sapience*, Vol. 1, p. 265 (Tr. 2, Part 2, ch. 7, sec. 8), and Vol. 2, p. 183 (Tr. 3, Part 4, ch. 1, sec. 7), citing Conference XXIII, 5–9, which it resembles.

52   Baker, *La Sainte Sapience*, Vol. 1, p. 260 (Tr. 3, Part 2, ch. 7, sec. 2), citing Conference XXIII, 6, 1–5. Like the preceding, this citation is made without references.

53   Baker, *La Sainte Sapience*, Vol. 1, pp. 74–5 (Tr. 1, Part 2, ch. 4, sec. 3), citing *RB* 73, 2: 'sunt doctrinae sanctorum Patrum', a phrase which follows, a few lines later, the mention of the 'Collationes Patrum et Instituta'; Vol. 1, p. 136 (Tr. 1, Part 3, ch. 4, sec. 5), alluding to *RB* 42, 3–5 and 73, 5.

54   Baker, *La Sainte Sapience*, Vol. 2, pp. 34–5 (Tr. 3, Part 1, ch. 4, sec. 9). Baker opposes there 'vocal prayers' and contemplative prayer. For him, the former represents the choir office recited by the monks of his time, that is to say without any pause for prayer between the psalms. He does not consider that the Egyptian cenobites practiced post-psalm prayer (cf. Institutes 11, 10–11), and that Cassian shows the prayer of post-psalm prayer (cf. Institutes 11, 10, 1; cf. Conference IX, 26, 1–2). On this fundamental element of the office, which we have scarcely begun to rediscover, see finally our article 'Psalmodie et prière: Remarques sur l'office de Saint Benoît', *Coll. Cist.* 44 (1982), 274–92.

8

LIVING HERE AND NOW

Spirituality in a Global Village

Laurence Freeman

A few weeks before John Main died he became increasingly confined to his bed. One day when I went into his room I was shocked to see the bed empty. A hundred thoughts ran through my mind but then I saw him collapsed on the floor on the other side of the bed. He had fallen while trying to get to the bathroom on his own. As I helped him back I saw he had cut his forehead and was bleeding from the small wound there. I was more shaken than he was and as he settled back into bed I said, 'Well, we'll probably laugh about this later.' He replied, 'Why don't we laugh about it now?' And so we did. Over the few weeks as he came closer to death I could see the cut on his head healing well day by day. It seemed bizarre that a dying man should have such good powers of recuperation. Why wasn't the body able to cure the cancer? There were other paradoxes that we lived intensely those weeks in the growing presence of the mystery of death. There was the paradox of living so intensely in the present moment and yet also at other times being aware of the hour-glass of his life running out so rapidly and visibly. There was the paradox of feeling joy and freedom in the midst of sadness and impending separation.

The way into reality as Fr John taught is through *paradox*.

In his chapter at the beginning of this book Charles Taylor alludes to the paradox that we have to humbly accept and acknow-

ledge in the religious consciousness of the modern world. It is
the paradox of being committed and rooted in a particular faith
while being also respectful and truly open to the truth or truths
of other faiths. In Taylor we witness a great philosophical intelligence arriving at the place of true worship, bowing before the
mystery that cannot be definitively understood, only entered. He
had discovered the apophatic dimension of knowledge – the way
of unknowing – that complements our more usual kataphatic
way of knowing through concepts and symbols. The Catholic
Church stated the same paradox when it said it rejected nothing that is true and holy in other faiths. Christ is united in his
universal salvific work to every human being but in 'a mysteri-
ous manner' – that is, not in a way that any institution or dogma
can define or control. The particularity and universality of Christ
– another facet of the paradox.

Living with paradox is distinctly uncomfortable. We like and
need security, predictability, and we prefer to have answers that
live with open-ended questions. Charles Taylor suggests that we
have simply to get used to this paradox in the modern world. Some
Buddhists speculate upon the possibility of there being multiple
absolute truths but they add: they don't know. The modern world
confronts us with many paradoxes thrown up by the rapidity of
change we are caught up in. Since the beginning of the industrial
age in the mid eighteenth century the world population has leapt
from 600 million to 6.6 billion. It continues to grow at the rate
of 70 to 80 million a year. Economic growth has reached an aver-
age of 5 per cent a year – not equally distributed of course. As we
know from the 25 per cent reduction in the Antarctic ice in the
past three years, there is a huge disparity between population and
economic growth which is reflected in the ecological crisis. The
dark paradox here is growth leading to death.

The environmental crisis makes us acutely aware that our
planet is a small place, interdependent and impermanent – the
defining characteristics of what the Buddhist calls emptiness

and the Christian understands as creation. An even odder paradox is that according to reputable economists the solution to this doom-watch is not so hard to solve. It requires about 1 per cent of the global economy, but also collaboration and a sense of unity, of being a human family rather than competing tribes. 'Our problems are man-made and can be solved by man,' President Kennedy said in 1961. Yet the USA continues to spend $600 billion on its military and to exploit terrorism as an excuse for polarizing world forces with antagonistic foreign and economic policies. Even at this time of the dissolving forces of capitalism we live in an age of rapid, relentless globalization and yet the hunger for difference and uniqueness has never been greater. The daughter of a meditator recently wrote that one of her top priorities in life was 'to be a local'. An interesting value to identify in an increasingly standardized 'global' world of internet, cheap travel, mass culture and virtual reality.

In all these ways the perennial paradox of the human condition seems to be more acutely felt by us as modern people than by our ancestors. Its extreme intensity and the lack of means of dealing with it through traditional religious and social securities has produced an age of anxiety, endemic stress, a mass consumerism driven by greed and riven with the fear of loneliness. To face this extreme confusion and suffering we have been forced to seek more deeply than ever the source and nature of meaning. Balfour Mount, in his chapter, explained with poignant examples and insights how death – the great paradox of all forms of life – can be a great teacher of meaning. In a way that confounds the modern consumer mind, happiness ('quality of life') evidently does not depend upon physical well-being or the satisfaction of desire. Suffering and joy do not exclude each other. We can die healed.

In the face of death the human mind becomes theological. We desperately seek meaning in order to avoid despair and we seek to express it in words we can share with others. The great loneliness of meaninglessness can be alleviated only by knowing that we understand each other even in the face of these cruel paradoxes of life. Sarah Bachelard explores the insight of the desert monks that prayer and theology – silence in God's mystery and speaking of that mystery – are both connected and mutually enriching. She finds in John Main's understanding of 'experience' and 'faith' a contribution to a new kind of language about ultimate meaning that many academic theologians still separate and divide. She exposes the crucial distinction between faith and belief that opens up true theology. This relieves us of the absurd self-contradiction of trying to believe what we are told we should believe and searching for an experience that will justify that belief. It frees us into the paradox of an experience that transcends 'experiences' and thus opens us to what Fr John called the fruits of the spirit manifested in our daily lives.

Yvon Théroux draws on the biblical prophets to illustrate how traditional and how revolutionary – itself a paradox that Charles Taylor exposes – is John Main's teaching on meditation as a way for modern people to live into and survive the intensely paradoxical nature of the world we live in today. Brian Johnstone explores the meaning of selfhood in the light of the mystical tradition that is John Main's context. From this sense of self as more than we can 'make' – rather, as what we receive and can bestow on others – the connection between meditation and the healing of human woundedness, whether social or psychological, becomes startlingly clear. Peter Ng speaks of how meditation is an integrated spirituality suited for redressing the dangerous human imbalance into which modern materialism and frantic busyness pushes so many. When he speaks of his prioritization of time and the ways he defends himself from losing the balancing mechanism of meditation I am reminded of something Augustine Baker wrote in the book that inspired Fr John to recover the tradition that we practise and teach in The World Community today. Baker was writing for enclosed Benedictine nuns whose chaplain he was, but he also insisted that lay people outside the monastery could also live a contemplative life if they chose to. They did not need to enter a cloister or take monastic vows in order to be contemplative. Of course, he said, there would be some necessary adjustments to their lifestyle, including – as Peter discovered – less going out for dinners and cocktail parties. Less going out in order to serve a deeper going in.

These are diverse but complementary reflections on the way John Main's teaching has radiated and expanded into the modern world and its issues. I would like now to draw together some of these themes of paradox, theology, tradition, healing and spirituality by reflecting on an important aspect of the central mystery of meditation as Fr John and the Christian mystical tradition have described it – the meaning of presence and the present moment, living here and now.

Let me begin by reminding you of how deeply inserted Fr John's teaching is in this tradition. This was affirmed soon after his death by the greatest living scholar of early monastic history and the author of one of the most radical commentaries on the Rule of St Benedict, Dom Adalbert de Vogüé, monk of the abbey of La Pierre qui Vire, who was born two years before John Main. De Vogue read Fr John's *Gethsemani Talks*[1] and recognized that it described a recovery of a tradition that Western monasticism had lost. He even said that it filled a gap in the Rule itself – the lack of a specific teaching on a method of the prayer of the heart.

> The role of mediator played by Cassian in Main's story is interesting in several ways. First of all, in the historical dimension it offers an example of having recourse to a pre-Benedictine author to enrich and correct the post-Benedictine tradition. As Baker had already done – but somewhat differently, as we shall see – Main returns to a source of the Rule to supply for a lacuna in it which is left open or imperfectly filled by those who make use of it.

In another dimension, that of space, this story unexpectedly continues the great mission of mediator which fell to Cassian. From their first appearance the invaluable service rendered by the Institutes and Conferences had been to transmit to the West a wisdom which was Egyptian, Oriental and Greek. In the case of Main this meeting between East and West expands beyond the Christian East to include the pagan Far-East.[2]

As Cassian bridges Eastern and Western Christianity, Main (de Vogue says) establishes a bridge between the Christian and non-Christian worlds. Latin monasticism, he goes on, had

> been deprived of any formula of prayer and that is why Conference X stands as a witness of such high importance. In fact only this teaching of Abbot Isaac reminds the monks of the West of a method of perpetual prayer which they have not been able to put into practice. It is a bitter paradox that the most ancient testimony of such a practice is in Latin and that it has been completely neglected by the Latin world. But Main's example shows that the foundation laid by Cassian was not in vain. Thanks to the author of the Conferences the *monologistos* prayer, as it was to be called by the monks of the East, belongs for ever to the treasury of the Western tradition, and nothing prevents the sons of St. Benedict from drawing it from there for their own profit, among the other *nova et vetera*.[3]

De Vogüé attests to what he calls 'Main's absolute Christian authenticity'. He was writing 25 years ago when many could not see the rootedness of Fr John's teaching in the tradition. Today this affirmation is less necessary as the Community has effectively done its work of educating the Christian churches with increasing effectiveness. The influence of John Main has now penetrated deeply into the mind of modern Christianity and awakened what seems now a much more obvious sense of the contemplative dimension of faith.

Charles Taylor reminds us of the original meaning of the word 'revolution' – going back to the beginning – and of the conviction of the early modern revolutionaries that they were restoring an 'original' state of affairs. John Main once spoke of the paradox of social revolution, that it always failed and led to a relapse into the very thing it had tried to escape. The only sustainable revolution, he concluded, is conversion of the heart. It is achieved not by force or by external action but by a radical turning of attention from self to the mystery of God. This alone leads to permanent and irreversible change – what he and the tradition calls the human destiny of *theosis*, divinization.

This now indicates why meditation can be seen as responding to the modern need for a global spirituality. This is not the same as a global religion or any kind of reductionistic new ageism. A global religion would lose too many local riches. A healthy, acceptable globalization must incorporate in a literally 'catholic' way everything that is local. A global spirituality, therefore, expresses a common element of all human religious experience, a foundation of radical human transformation and an opportunity to respond in unity to the complexity of modern global paradoxes. Meditation connects the global to the local because it connects the individual to the family, the heart to the mind, the inner to the outer.

The paradox is that, in the light of this spirituality, the words, symbols and concepts of the different religious traditions can become unifying differences rather than threatening divisions. Yet – an even deeper paradox – these words, thoughts and images must be shattered if they are to do their work of uniting us. C. S. Lewis said that 'all reality is iconoclastic' and in *A Grief Observed* he applied this universal truth to the particularity of his Christian faith when, dealing with his bereavement after the death of his wife, he said he needed Christ not something that resembles Christ.

Even a very good photograph, he said, might in the end become a snare, a horror or obstacle to a true 'remembering' of a loved one who had died.

It was death – the loss of his wife – that taught Lewis this meaning of faith. John Main, like all of us, also learned it through the many experiences of separation that marked his life. But in meditation he applied this truth to the inner journey and related the very meaning of prayer to a 'smashing of the mirror' of the ego-mind. This is an unusually strong image in his teaching where he prefers to speak of polishing, harmonizing, uniting, connecting. But he did not underestimate the discipline and asceticism involved in this spirituality. There is a good side to the hard work, though. He also believed that once we have begun the pilgrimage of daily meditation we have found the essential ascesis of human life. This discovery freed him from the scrupulosity of so many religious people about how and where to control or deny their desires. In a contemplative vision of life you can enjoy the good things of life with a good conscience. Like the rabbi who said we would be held to account on the last day for every legitimate pleasure we did not accept, John Main believed in living life to the full. Once you have started to say the mantra, the meaning of Augustine's great affirmation of Christian freedom becomes clearer: 'Love and do what you like.'

The mirror we smash is the consequence of the fall, the meaning of sin, because it is the divided mind, the separation of consciousness from its sources, the prison and hellishly infinite regression of the ego's self-reflection. Smashing the mirror transforms what Fr John calls the 'silence of oblivion' into the 'silence of full consciousness'. Meditation as a work of silence smashes the mirror by detaching us from every image and thought.

In other talks, delivering the same message with different tools, he spoke of meditation as a process of self-discovery and self-knowledge. According to the Christian mystical tradition self-knowledge is more than ideas about ourselves. It is an experiential insight into the deepest nature of our self in which we discover that we are – both individually and collectively – a microcosm of the created universe. This is why meditation becomes a spirituality that speaks so directly to modern concerns and offers a way forward to the solution of global problems. In finding out who we are we find the solution to all those forces that seem to alienate us from our true selves. The solution to our complex modern problems, Fr John said, must in the end be spiritual. As Gregory of Nyssa said, 'You have within yourself the standard by which to apprehend the divine.' The paradoxical relation of the universal and the particular is resolved by entering the mystery of God which dwells within us and among us. The Kingdom of God is non-dual, wave and particle, interior and exterior, solitary and communal.

Meditation creates community out of the energy of paradox. In the light of the experience of meditation we see ourselves and others as united and no longer as alienated. We are then free to act on the basis of what we really see.

This global spirituality has many other aspects which the consistent but multifaceted teaching of Fr John explores. The aspect which he returns to most often is that of love – the most universal of human values and source of meaning. It is also the central paradox in which we lose in order to find, let go in order to own. Love has a trinitarian dynamic even in the early human stages of its development into the fullness of agape. In Eros and in Friendship, in family or romantic love, in social justice and personal compassion we discover that love of self, love of others and love of God are distinct but inseparable. Fr John's psychological insight and compassion led him to reverse the usual religiously sanctioned sequence of love. He placed the love of self first because how can we love others when we are still locked into self-rejection or self-hatred? How can we love the God we cannot see unless we love the brothers and sisters that we can see?

Another aspect of this universal spirituality that Fr John recognized in Christian terms is liberty. Above all it is the liberty to love, to be, rather than just the freedom to choose, to do what we fancy doing. For Fr John fear is the great constraint and meditation frees us from fear and liberates us into the 'liberty of the children of God'. His language on this aspect of meditation reflects that of the early fathers – like Clement of Alexandria, who said that, 'We are no longer under the law which was accompanied by fear but under the Word, the master of free choice.'[4] Here in Christian terms is that freedom from addiction and from the prison of the divided self that the 12-step programme has made conscious for many. It is the intoxicating expansion of mind and heart that Bal Mount and Victor Frankl call 'meaning' and that Patricia Ng was led to in her last illness, through meditation, faith and deep human love and why she said in such radiantly simple words of authentic enlightenment: 'I have learned the secret of happiness is to leave everything in God's hands and trust in his great care for us.'[5] Or what Eileen O'Hea saw and says in her poem 'On Enlightenment (My Version)':

> I wonder,
>   have for some time,
> if consciousness, heightened consciousness,
>   is enlightenment,
> and, if so,
>   what relationship
>   does it have with Wisdom?

> I had thought
>   enlightenment was a prize –
>   the reward of a good life.
> You know,
>   the fasting, self-denied life;
>   the beating the be-jibes
>   out of your ego life!

To me, it seems,
Wisdom is a sitter.
You meet her
   at the center of your soul.
Like a salmon swimming up stream
   you strive and strive,
      then flop,
you are sitting in her lap.

Here, Wisdom gathers
the energies of consciousness,
like eggs in a nest,
and sits with them,
   mothering, fathering them
   in Her silent presence –
a presence of light.

Soaked
   in Wisdom's light,
energy moves out again
into the stream of life,
creating a presence,
   like fireflies
   on the blackest of nights.[6]

The central aspect of the spirituality of meditation – or rather
the spirituality that is meditation because, as Fr John insisted,
meditation is not just a method of prayer but a way of life – is
time. Christian faith is founded on the incarnation of the eternal
Word in the historical person of Jesus. The theological expansion on this theme has been immense and continues to expand.
The mind can never finish wondering at it. Maximus the Con-
fessor said that there are three manifestations of the Word – in
the Cosmos as Being, in the personal mystery of God and in the

historical figure of Jesus. Fr John teaches meditation from this faith-apprehension of the mystery of Christ but he most often approaches it from the transformed, daily experience of time that results from the practice. This is the kind of *experience* in faith that Sarah Bachelard writes of and it is the new way of looking at life that Peter Ng was describing in the life of a busy executive.

In an age of stress and anxiety like ours the mystery of time presses heavily upon us. Without meaning, the intolerable weight of time and, paradoxically, its fleeting disappearance become a crucifixion without a resurrection. The great increase in the incidence of mental illness in modern society could be attributed to this. Meditation transforms our mental construct of past and future by deepening the experience of the present moment – the core meaning of contemplation as the 'simple enjoyment of the truth', as Aquinas defines it.

Death, which marvellously concentrates the mind, leads us to a heightened experience of reality. Every precious moment is tasted and shared with wonder and joy. Lovers facing death enjoy every moment together that is left to them, but they are not counting the seconds. The present moment cannot be measured. This too is freedom from limits. The waitress who says 'enjoy' as you start your meal sometimes has it right. Eat, drink and be merry when appropriate. How can we describe the present moment except with reference to time? We cannot, just as we cannot speak of the one Word without using words. But the present moment is not separate from what we imagine as past and future. It contains time. We could say that the present moment is experienced when we stop counting or watching the seconds ticking away. It dawns when we truly see that the present moment is literally *every* moment, successive to the degree of being unbroken and without any moment being blinked at, wasted, forgotten or ignored. It is about being fully awake to everything. Here and now.

This is the last paradox to give us a headache in this chapter. How can time and eternity coexist? Yet meditation – practised seriously as Fr John would say – shows us that we can live in the eternal now while writing reports about yesterday's meetings and planning our meetings for tomorrow. Healing can take place as we are dying. One can understand why the Vedic tradition so dramatizes all this when it says that this world is all illusion, just a dream world we will awake from like watching a film on a screen and then turning on the lights and turning the projector off. Fr John and the Christian tradition don't like to say this because it diminishes the paradox of the incarnation as well as the experience of human love from day to day and over the years of our life's pilgrimage. Yet in the light of the present moment so much of our thoughts and assumptions are exposed as illusory, so many anxieties evaporate, so many crises disappear and so many of our hang-ups seem to be released. Yet Fr John does not minimize the purification of the mind that must first take place:

> But this we must understand too. I would mislead you seriously if I didn't put before you as clearly as I can. The purification that leads to this purity of heart that leads to the presence within us is a consuming fire. And meditation is entering that fire. The fire that burns away everything that is not real, that burns away everything that is not true, that is not loving. We must not be afraid of the fire. We must have absolute confidence in the fire for the fire is the fire of love. The fire is even more – this is the great mystery of our faith – it is the fire *who* is love.[7]

Say your mantra. If we truly say it we can be nowhere else but here and now. Our attention positions us in the embodied reality of God and reveals that attention itself is love and that our attention to God is really the same as God's attention to us. 'It is all love', as Fr John wrote once in a letter to someone struggling with the difficulty of paradox in their life. It is too simple to practice – so we think, just as the disciples thought, 'it was too good to be true' when they saw the risen Jesus. But when we stop thinking about it the simplicity becomes easy, natural and effortless. The challenge is to persevere through the long struggle with distraction, thinking that the distraction is so important. Thinking that thinking is so powerful that it blocks us from being. Not realizing that the present moment is present even when we are distracted and lost in anxiety or fantasy. Our attention to it is efficacious even if we seem to be distant from it. At times, and increasingly, the present moment is realized (not achieved or gained) in those moments where faith and grace combine in perfect ease and thought subsides into the silence of full consciousness. Later, of course, we think about it and maybe ask if this is a real experience, and the clouds form again and we lose the view. But we know it is there. We cannot forget the present moment.

This simple, direct awareness of present reality which expands in silence, stillness and simplicity, and to which the faithful attention to the mantra leads us, is what John Main knew and taught us about. It explains his human qualities – love and compassion, kindness, gentleness, patience, fidelity, humour and liberty of spirit. But, even more important, it also explains how he taught, wishing us to know it for ourselves in our own experience, rather than trying to describe it or by focusing our attention on his personality or his own experience in meditation.

It is so simple and yet so transformative. Fr John believed with a passion that meditation needed to be taught so as to lead people into the fullness of life, into the present moment. If we look together at our overwhelming global problems whose magnitude drive so many to addiction or self-alienation, if we look at them in the unclouded beauty and joy of the present moment, if we approach them with the peace that passes all thought, the way forward will seem so obvious, so equally simple, that we will laugh at ourselves for getting into them in the first place and even more for thinking for so long they were insoluble.

Laurence Freeman

Notes

1 John Main, *Christian Meditation: The Gethsemani Talks*, 3rd edn, London, Continuum, 2000.

2 Adalbert de Vogüé, 'From John Cassian to John Main', *Monastic Studies*, 1984, pp. 89–94 (see Chapter 7 of this book).

3 de Vogüé, 'From John Cassian to John Main'.

4 Clement of Alexandria, *The Instructor*, Book 1, ch. 6.

5 From the film, *From Panic to Peace*, Singapore, Medio Media, 2005.

6 Eileen O'Hea, 'On Enlightenment (My Version)', in *The World Community Christian Meditation Newsletter*, International edn, Vol. 31, No. 4, December 2007.

7 John Main, *Door to Silence*, London, Canterbury Press, 2006, p. 9.

CONTRIBUTORS

Sarah Bachelard

Sarah Bachelard is an Anglican priest and lecturer in theology at St Mark's National Theological Centre in Canberra, Australia. She studied theology with Rowan Williams at Oxford University on a Rhodes Scholarship, and spent a year at the Graduate Theological Union in Berkeley before doing her doctorate in moral philosophy at the Australian National University. She was Associate Director of the John Main Center for Meditation and Inter-Religious Dialogue at Georgetown University from January to May 2006. She has a particular interest in how the practice of meditation can be a source of deep renewal in the Church and in the relationship between contemplation and ethical life.

Adalbert de Vogüé

Adalbert de Vogüé has been called the greatest modern commentator on the life and Rule of Saint Benedict. Born in 1924, he entered the monastery of Ste-Marie de La Pierre-qui-Vire in France in 1944. In 1959, he gained his doctorate in theology in Paris. Since 1974, he has lived in a hermitage close to the monastery. He is the author of numerous scholarly books and articles, mostly in French, but many have been translated into English: *To Desire Eternal Life* (2002), *Reading St. Benedict* (1994), *Life of St. Benedict* (1993), *Rule of St. Benedict: A Doctrinal and Spiritual Commentary* (1983), and the two-volume set of *Community and Abbot In the Rule of St. Benedict* (1978–79).

Laurence Freeman

Laurence Freeman is a Benedictine monk of the Olivetan Congregation, Director of The World Community for Christian Meditation and spiritual successor to John Main, whom he helped in establishing the first Christian Meditation Centre in London in 1975. Laurence Freeman is the author of many books and articles, including *Light Within, Selfless Self, Web of Silence, Common Ground, A Short Span of Days, Your Daily Practice* and *Jesus: The Teacher Within*. He has conducted dialogues and peace initiatives, such as the historic Way of Peace with the Dalai Lama, and he is active in dialogue with other faiths as well as in encouraging the teaching of Christian meditation to children and students and the recovery of the contemplative wisdom tradition in the Church and society at large.

Brian V. Johnstone

Brian Johnstone is a moral theologian and member of the Canberra Province of Redemptorists in Australia. He taught in Rome for 20 years, most recently at the Alphonsian Academy of the Pontifical Lateran University. He currently holds the Warren Blanding Chair of Religion and Culture at the Catholic University of America in Washington DC, where he is specializing in bioethics, moral theology and the 'Philosophy of the Gift', a project extending the philosophical and ethical concept of giving a 'gift' to a new framework for moral theology, by defining the ultimate and absolutely gratuitous gift of self as that of Jesus Christ on the cross, completed in the resurrection.

Balfour M. Mount

Balfour Mount is a Canadian physician, surgeon and academic. He is considered to be the father of palliative care in Canada and the USA, and he has been vastly influential in his field worldwide. He was the founding Director of the Royal Victoria Hospital Palliative Care Services in Montreal. Dr Mount was John Main's personal physician and has been a friend of The World Community for Christian Meditation from its inception at New Harmony in 1991 when he became the first chairperson of the WCCM Guiding Board. Mount led the John Main Seminar 'On Wholeness' in 1989. He was named an Officer of the Order of Canada in 2003 and of the Ordre National du Québec in 1988.

Peter Ng

Peter Ng is Chief Investment Officer of the Singapore Government Investment Corporation, and a Trustee and Guiding Board member of the WCCM. He is the national co-ordinator of the Christian Meditation Community in Singapore, which he co-founded with his late wife, Patricia, in 1988. He has edited many books and audio productions for the WCCM, including the recent book and CD set based on John Main's recorded talks, named *The Hunger for Depth and Meaning*. He is also the producer and editor of the quarterly *Meditatio* CDs which are distributed to Christian meditation groups worldwide. He is the author of the Meditatio CD *The Contemplative Executive – Leading from the Heart*, in which he explores the value of Christian meditation for business people.

Charles Taylor

One of the most important thinkers Canada has produced, Charles Taylor was a pupil of Isaiah Berlin at Oxford. He is currently Professor Emeritus at McGill University in Montreal. Charles Taylor led the John Main Seminar in 1988 and has been close to the Christian Meditation Community from its beginning. He was winner of the Templeton Prize in 2007 for progress towards research of discoveries about spiritual realities, and in June 2008 he was awarded the Kyoto Prize, sometimes referred to as the Japanese Nobel, for Lifetime Achievement in the Arts and Philosophy category. His writings have been translated into 20 languages, and have covered a range of subjects that include artificial intelligence, language, social behaviour, morality and multiculturalism. His latest book, *A Secular Age*, has won many awards including Times Literary Supplement Book of the Year 2008.

Yvon Théroux

Yvon Théroux is Professor at the Collège André-Grasset in Montreal, a lecturer in the Department of Religious Sciences at the University of Quebec at Montreal and a former Chair of Méditation Chrétienne du Québec. He began his career as a professor of biology but his work has involved theology, education, science of religion, gerontology and bioethics. He is also a much published researcher on religious experience and neuroscience and his latest book, co-authored with Patrick Rajotte, is *La Spiritualité Amérindienne* (2004).

THE WORLD COMMUNITY FOR CHRISTIAN MEDITATION

The World Community for Christian Meditation took form in 1991. It continues John Main's legacy in teaching Christian meditation and his work of restoring the contemplative dimension of Christian faith in the life of the Church.

The Community is now directed by Laurence Freeman OSB, a student of John Main and a Benedictine monk of the Olivetan Congregation. The World Community has its International Centre and a retreat centre in London. There are a number of Centres in other parts of the world. The Community is thus a 'monastery without walls', a family of national communities and emerging communities in over a hundred countries. The foundation of this Community is the local meditation group, which meets weekly in homes, parishes, offices, hospitals, prisons and colleges. The World Community works closely with many Christian churches.

Annually it runs the John Main Seminar and The Way of Peace. It also sponsors retreats, schools for the training of teachers of meditation, seminars, lectures and other programmes. It contributes to interfaith dialogues, particularly in recent years with Buddhists and Muslims. A quarterly spiritual letter with news of the Community is mailed and also available online. Weekly readings can be sent direct by email. Information on current programmes, connections to national co-ordinators and the location of meditation groups can be found on the Community website (www.wccm.org), which also offers a range of online audio talks. This site is the hub of a growing family of internet presence, the websites of national communities and special interests, such as the teaching of meditation to children and the contemporary spirituality of priests.

Medio Media is the communication and publishing arm of The World Community and offers a wide range of books, audio and videos to support the practice of meditation. The online bookstore is at www.mediomedia.org.

Contact details for WCCM centres worldwide

International Centre
The World Community for Christian Meditation
St Mark's
Myddelton Square
London EC1R 1XX
UK

Tel: +44 20 7278 2070
Fax: +44 20 7713 6346
email: welcome@wccm.org
www.wccm.org

For countries not listed below contact the International Centre

Argentina
email: malen_puebla@hotmail.com
www.meditacioncristiana_argentina

Australia
email: leon@christianmeditationaustralia.org
www.christianmeditationaustralia.org

Belgium
email: jose.pype@skynet.be
www.christmed.be

Brazil
email: ana.fonseca@umusic.com
www.wccm.com.br

Canada
email: christianmeditation@bellnet.ca
www.meditatio.ca

email: medchre@bellnet.ca
www.meditationchretienne.ca

Chile
email: mr_meditacion@yahoo.es
www.meditacioncristiana.cl

The World Community for Christian Meditation

China
email: wccm.hongkong@gmail.com
www.wccm.hk

Czech Republic
email: info@krestanskameditace,cz
www.krestanskameditace.com

Fiji
email: denisemc@connect,com.fj

France
email: cmmc@wanadoo.fr
www.meditationchretienne.org

Germany
email: dirk.grosser@wccm.de
www.wccm.de

Haiti
email: inobert@yahoo.fr

Hong Kong
email: wccm.hongkong@gmail.com
www.wccm.hk

India Christian Meditation Centre
email: jpst_1995@yahoo.co.uk

Indonesia
email: lucia_gani@yahoo.com
www.meditasikristiani.com

Ireland
email: sylviathompson@eircom.net
www.wccmireland.org

Italy
email: wccmitalia@virgilio.it
www.meditazionecristiana.org

Latvia
email: george@animalibra.lv
www.jesus.lv

Malaysia
email: wccm.malaysia@gmail.com

Malta
www.wccmalta.org

Mexico
email: lucia_gayon@yahoo.com
www.meditacioncristiana.com

Netherlands
email: cm_nederland@hotmail.com
www.wccm.nl

New Zealand Christian Meditation Community
email: ccm@ihug.co.nz

Norway
email: asemarku@hotmail.com
email: wccmnorge@live.no

Philippines
email: czgomez123@yahoo.com

Poland
email: paulina_szczecin@wccm.pl
www.wccm.pl

Portugal
email: mcristinags@netcabo.pt

Singapore
email: daulet@pacific.net.sg

South Africa
email: ansjohan@eject.co.za
www.wccm.co.za

The World Community for Christian Meditation

Sri Lanka
email: aloma@dplgroup.com

Switzerland
email: deborah.walton@gmail.com

United Kingdom
email: uk@wccm.org
www.christian-meditation.org.uk

USA
email: gbebeau@gmail.com
www.wccm-usa.org

Venezuela
email: asosa@CAF.com
www.meditadores.blogspot.com

West Indies
email: ruthsjc@wow.net